Positively Birmingham

Jonathan Berg

BPL

Birmingham Picture Library

First Published in 1994 by
Birmingham Picture Library
14 St Bernard's Road, Olton, Solihull, B92 7BB
Tel: 0121-765-4114 Fax: 0121-765-4224

Second edition 1997

ISBN 0 9523179 5 8

British Library Cataloguing in Publication Data
A catalogue record for this book is available from the British
Library.

Design and Typesetting by John Williams,
The Image Foundry, Cambridge.

Printed by Piggott Printers Limited, Cambridge.

Contents

Page numbers for photographs are shown in bold in the index.

Foreword

Once upon a time, and it wasn't so long ago, you couldn't even buy a postcard of Birmingham. In fact it was impossible for those of us who lived in and around Birmingham to find anything that depicted our city at all. This helped perpetuate the tired old cliché that Birmingham was a dirty, dark, industrial hole in the ground, whose only notable feature was Spaghetti Junction.

Birmingham is the proud home of the 'Brummies' - an affectionate term for the people of Birmingham. Unlike many other towns and cities, you don't have to be born here to be one of us. You just have to *want* to be a Brummie, and in no time at all you'll find yourself accepted as one.

And what a mix we are! Those of us who weren't actually born here have settled from all over the world. This place grows on you and in no time at all Birmingham has captured you in its warm and welcoming web. But how do we convey our pride and affection to those who don't live here?

Enter Jonathan Berg. In 1994 he published the first edition of this book. The then Lord Mayor, the legendary Sir Richard Knowles, greeted the work as 'the sort of gift any Birmingham man or woman can give to friends and that can be presented by the many successful Birmingham businesses to valued customers'. The book was a milestone. Contemporary Birmingham simply hadn't been depicted in such a comprehensive way before. Locals and visitors alike reacted with great enthusiasm to its publication.

Three years later *Positively Birmingham* has been updated to reflect a great city heading proudly towards the millennium.

If you are new to Birmingham, this is the best reminder of our beautiful City that you can buy. And I should know. We journalists never lie.

If you have received this book as a gift from a

loved one in Birmingham, it's a trick. We are trying to seduce you here, if only for a visit.

But if you know Birmingham well, either as a resident or regular visitor, you will truly appreciate the love and care that has gone into making *Positively Birmingham* worthy of this second edition - and many more to come.

Ed Doolan
BBC Radio, Pebble Mill
April 1997

Preface to the First Edition

In 1990 I began to fulfil a long-standing ambition, by starting work on a book of photography of contemporary Birmingham. It was more luck than judgement that this coincided with such a dynamic time in the development of the city. Some major civic projects have now been completed, and this is an excellent time to reflect on the results of all this activity.

This book, then, contains the images of one Birmingham photographer. It is about things that have caught my imagination, and prompted me to explore further in today's city. The text aims to set the photographs in context, adding my personal feelings for this place.

For those interested in the technical side, most of the photographs were taken using a Bronica ETRS medium format camera. For architectural shots a Gandolfi 4" x 5" camera was used.

Birmingham is a complex city with an enormous number of different facets and it has been interesting for me to learn more about it as this book has developed, but of course there are many aspects not covered here. I hope that *Positively Birmingham* will give a feel for what I find a great city in which to live and work.

Jonathan Berg

July 1994.

Preface to the Second Edition

Birmingham continues to approach the future in a single-minded way. Much has been accomplished in the city since the first edition of *Positively Birmingham* and this is reflected in additional material and photographs in this second edition.

There are many books about Birmingham's past but one can spend too much time being nostalgic. *Positively Birmingham* is more about the present, dipping into the city's history to explain and set in context what you can experience today.

Jonathan Berg

April 1997

Acknowledgements

This new edition of *Positively Birmingham* has been made possible because of the enthusiasm for the first edition from Birmingham bookshops and the general public. Those who promote the city and Birmingham businesses have also encouraged me to produce this second edition. Thanks to you all.

Sylvia Platt kindly cast her editorial eye over changes for the second edition and Marjorie Elliot also looked through the text for errors. I appreciate the continuing friendship and professionalism of Mike Cartwright, John Williams and the rest of the team at The Image Foundry and Piggott Printers.

JDB, April 1997

▶

*The Head Post Office
which dates from 1891.
In the 1970s the Victorian
Society mounted a successful
campaign to stop the
demolition of this building.*

Chapter One
Victoria Square

Victoria Square is an excellent place to start this photographic exploration of Birmingham. It both possesses some of Birmingham's finest Victorian buildings, and demonstrates the city's determination to revitalise itself for the future. Let us consider the Victorian architecture and the contemporary public art of this fascinating place.

With the complete restoration of Victoria Square in 1993, our Victorian ancestors' dream of this area as a grand civic space was finally realised. At the beginning of the 1990s Victoria Square was dominated by busy roads; on her plinth Queen Victoria surveyed the scene, though with bustling traffic all around, this was no place for a commoner to linger.

Classical Designs

The impressive Town Hall was designed by the architects Hansom and Welch, who won the architectural competition for its design in 1832. Joseph Hansom is perhaps better remembered for the Hansom Cab. The project was beset with financial problems, ending with bankruptcy for

Victoria Square Opening.
The sun was out for the official opening of Victoria Square by the Princess of Wales on 6 May 1993.

▶

The River
(Dhruva Mistry, 1993) is the focal point of Victoria Square.

▼

▲

Victoria Square
as it was in 1990.

the architects and with the Birmingham architect Edge completing the work. Although opened in 1834, the Town Hall was not finally complete until 1850. Constructed from Anglesey marble in a classical design based on the temple of Castor and Pollux in the Forum in Rome, it towered above the surroundings and influenced the design of the Victorian buildings which were to follow.

The Town Hall has played a part in some important historical events. The Chartist Movement, which promoted Parliamentary reform, was very powerful in the city, split between those favouring peaceful reform and those prepared to consider violent demonstrations. When Chartist riots broke out in 1839, the Town Hall was used as the headquarters for a two-thousand-strong special constabulary brought in to quell the uprising.

In 1901 at a meeting on the Boer War in the Town Hall, David Lloyd George, then a young Liberal MP, was prevented from speaking by a mob who gathered outside and began breaking windows. He is said to have escaped by borrowing a policeman's uniform and marching out of the hall as part of a police squad.

▶

Iron Man
(Antony Gormley, 1993).
Produced from 3/4" cast-iron
plates, buried up to its calves
and leaning to the side and
back, this work simply cannot
be ignored.

The Council House

The Council House is closely linked to Joseph Chamberlain and to the great municipal changes of the late nineteenth century. As Mayor of Birmingham, Chamberlain laid the foundation stone to the Council House on 14 June 1874, an event celebrated with a luncheon and fireworks in Aston Park. Yeoville Thomason, who had previously designed buildings in Colmore Row, won the competition for the Council House design amid much controversy and recrimination among the members of the council. The main façade has a mosaic by Salviati and sculptures including *Britannia Rewarding the Manufacturers of Birmingham* in the middle. The open space created in front was first known as Council House Square but when a statue of Queen Victoria was installed in 1901 it was renamed Victoria Square.

The Head Post Office, a Turning Point

Redevelopment of Birmingham City Centre in the 1960s and 1970s saw a number of fine Victorian buildings demolished to make way for the new civic buildings and the inner ring road. Campaigns were launched by the Victorian Society to try to save a number of buildings, successful in the case of the French Renaissance-style Head Post Office in Victoria Square. This has been redeveloped (completed in 1991) and is now a high quality office block offering a modern environment in an historic setting. In 1973 permission had been granted to demolish the building and it was only vigorous campaigning by the Victorian Society members which saved this historic building. This proved to be a turning point in Victorian conservation in Birmingham. Adjacent to the Post Office, Number 1 Victoria Square is a modern office development, completed in 1985 on the site of the old Parcels Office, and fortunately, after further pressure from conservationists, modified at the planning stage to ensure that it was in keeping with surrounding buildings.

Lisa Clayton spent eight months sailing single-handed around the world. On her return the 'Spirit of Birmingham' had pride of place in Victoria Square and Lisa was available to meet the people.

▼

Cooling off in Victoria Square. ▶

In August 1995 Victoria Square saw celebrations to mark fifty years of peace. ▶

Christmas celebrations in 1996 included a mural on the Town Hall. ▼

◀

Ebony, the Victoria Square site dog got dressed up for the EC Summit and is seen here with Mick Mulligan. Ebony was introduced to the Princess of Wales at the opening of the Square and a paw print can be seen in the paving close to the Queen Victoria statue.

Setting the jets on The River *in April 1993.*

▶

The Re-Making of Victoria Square

In August 1991 major changes to transform the city centre were announced. A pedestrianisation scheme with Victoria Square as a focal point was proposed, incorporating the space defined by the Town Hall, Council House, Head Post Office and top of New Street. The nineteenth-century buildings around Victoria Square are in marked contrast to the twentieth-century backdrop to Centenary Square, which was completed just as plans for Victoria Square became a reality. The statue of Queen Victoria and other important architectural and artistic features of the Square, notably the Council House and Town Hall, have all been renovated and restored using the original stone.

Victoria Square Sculptures

Contemporary pieces of sculpture in the Square by Dhruva Mistry are sympathetic to their surroundings with their use of the traditional materials water, stone and bronze. Born in 1957 and brought up in India, Mistry studied sculpture at the University of Baroda and the Royal College

The Queen Victoria Statue with the Princess of Wales.

▼

of Art, had a residency at Kettle's Yard, Cambridge and was recently elected a Royal Academian. He explains his work as follows:

> *The central feature of* The River, *a monumental bronze fountain figure, is a metaphor for life source. It sits in a sandstone shell upheld by a group of encircling salmon. Eleven radiating water-jets punctuate the overflow of water from the shell into the upper pool.*

> *White-water springs forth from the hands of the River and cascades down the weir into the lower pool fountain of the* Youth. *The honeysuckle shaped fountain appears to float in the middle of the pool surrounded by four basic shapes on the floor; a cube, cone, cylinder and sphere. A boy and girl sit on the cube and cylinder respectively in a mood of quiet reflection.*

> *The* Victoria Square Guardians *are two large sphinx-like images as composite creatures, carved from Darley Dale sandstone, and which look over the lower pool piazza. These sculptures are symbolic protectors of the peace, pride and dignity of the square.*

> *The* Object-Variations, *a pair of sandstone lampposts, flank the river to create a spatial relationship of the works, in and around the water feature, as upholders of light for the entire installation.*

Centrally placed on the façade of the Council House is the sculptural relief, Britannia Rewarding the Manufacturers of Birmingham (Lockwood, Boulton and Sons).

▼

▲

*The Victoria Square
Guardians and city centre
office workers often
meet for lunch.*

The Iron Man

Outside the old Head Post Office in Victoria
Square is a cast-iron figure, twenty feet high,
buried up to its calves and tilted at an angle. The
ambiguity of this sculpture by Antony Gormley,
now known as *Iron Man*, invites speculation by the
viewer. The use of iron is a specific reference to
Birmingham's industrial history. Like *Forward* in
Centenary Square (page 97), *Iron Man* has aroused
strong feelings and has been the subject of considerable discussion, not all of it well informed.

Gas Lighting is Back

The redevelopment of Victoria Square has
included the laying of brick paving and York stone
flags. The Darley Dale sandstone used to build the
Council House in the 1870s and, recently, to restore
its façade was also used extensively in building the
Square.

A number of trees, specially imported from
Germany, have been planted in the Square and
these continue along Colmore Row. Four
Victorian-style gas lamps are the first gas street-
lighting in Birmingham city centre for over forty

years, and are partly sponsored by West Midlands Gas, to celebrate 200 years of gas lighting.

Victoria Square has been transformed into a major new focal point for the city. It now plays an important role in linking the commercial and shopping centres of the city with the redeveloped Broad Street and Centenary Square areas. In the dynamic era of Chamberlain's 'Municipal Revolution' in Birmingham the intention was to create a civic and cultural centre based on this square; now over 120 years later these aspirations have finally been accomplished and with considerable style.

St Nicholas's Church, King's Norton, was rebuilt in the 14th century from an earlier Norman chapel. The south porch dates from the 15th century and parish business was often conducted here. Note the remains of the foliage dripstone round the arch. Just visible on the left-hand side, below the angel, are remains of a 'Mass' dial, which was a special sundial showing the time of the next mass.

Chapter Two
Earlier Times

Reasons for the growth and development of Birmingham are complex and even learned historical texts are full of conjecture. Certainly Birmingham was not significant in Roman times - Metchley Camp, located on Birmingham University campus in Edgbaston, and the remains of a Roman road in Sutton Park are the only major relics from the Roman period. In the Domesday Book (1086) the manor of Birmingham was described as one of the poorest in the area.

A Marketplace

What gave rise to Birmingham's importance as a commercial and manufacturing centre? The city centre is built on a sandstone ridge between the rivers Tame and Rea. In the mid-twelfth century the hamlets around Birmingham needed a focus and in 1154 Peter de Bermingham, who controlled the Birmingham manor, seized an opportunity and was granted a market day for the town; this encouraged early growth and development.

The close proximity to the Black Country, an area to the north-west of Birmingham which was rich in raw materials, was an important factor in the growth of industry in the town. Equally important were access to cheap energy - originally river

Metchley Camp was a Roman camp. This preserved corner lies close to Birmingham University Medical School. In 1953 the site gained interest by the addition of a wooden reconstruction of the ramparts but little of this now remains.

By the middle of the 12th century the hamlets around Birmingham needed a trading centre. Birmingham took the initiative by obtaining a market charter from the Crown. To this day the Digbeth area of Birmingham is still very much a marketplace. Seen here are some of today's markets; the Fish Market, Flea Market and the Sunday morning car boot sale in the middle of the Wholesale Markets.

Birmingham as it is today. ▶

Birmingham city centre from Bordesley Village.
St Martin's Church is in the centre with the Bull Ring Centre just to the right. Other buildings that stand out include Bank House, the Hyatt Hotel, Alpha Tower and the Rotunda (from the left).

▼

water to drive mills and later coal - the supply of cheap labour, a growing demand for household products and the town's entrepreneurial spirit. Surges in industrial production during periods of war have also promoted the growth of manufacturing over the centuries.

A Collection of Hamlets

In the thirteenth century there were some forty to fifty hamlets within today's city boundary and the

The Old Crown, Deritend.
This is a timber-framed
medieval building, partly
originating from 1368 and
is thought to be the oldest
building in the city centre.

▶

remnants of life in these different parishes can be seen all over today's city - medieval churches in the Parishes of Sheldon, Aston, King's Norton and Yardley and half-timbered Grammar Schools at Yardley and King's Norton. Further examples of surviving ancient architecture include inns such as the Great Stone Inn at Northfield.

Half-Timbered Houses

During the reign of Henry VIII John Leland, a traveller, visited Birmingham. In 1538 he noted half-timbered houses and the parish church of St Martins, and saw that Birmingham was already involved in the metal trade, using iron and coal from the Black Country to produce items such as knives and nails in small forges and workshops. Buildings in the city centre from around this period include the Old Crown Inn in Digbeth High Street, and Stratford House at Camp Hill.

Surviving Old Buildings

The timber-framed Old Crown Inn, described by Leland as a 'mansion house of tymber', dates from

▲

Stratford House.
This is a superb building hidden away from the busy Stratford Road at Camp Hill. It was built in 1601 and restored in 1954.

◀

The Old Grammar School at Yardley.
Just one of many examples of the medieval past to be found in Birmingham's suburbs.

*The Old Grammar School
at King's Norton.
A medieval building dating
from the 15th century.
Originally it may have stood
on stilts, the ground floor
being added in the
16th century.*

▼

1368 and is the oldest building in the centre of Birmingham. Its frontage has changed little over the years.

Elizabethan and Jacobean buildings include Blakesley Hall at Yardley and, closer to the city centre, Stratford House at Camp Hill, originally built in 1601 as Ambrose Rotton's farm. From 1601 until the 1880s the house was in the ownership of just two families, the original Rottons and then the

St Nicholas's Church sits above the Canal House (1796) and junction of the Worcester and Birmingham and Stratford canals at King's Norton. ▶

Blakesley Hall is a yeoman's house dating from about 1550; it is open to the public and run by the Birmingham Museums and Arts. ▶

Simcox family. During the second part of the nineteenth century, as Birmingham rapidly expanded, the house became surrounded by back-to-back housing. In 1926 Stratford House was sold to the LMS Railway who threatened to demolish it to make space for a goods yard. However, they gave way to public pressure and the building remains standing, having been renovated in 1954 by Ivon Adams, and it is now used as offices.

Aston Hall and Park

During the late sixteenth and early seventeenth centuries a substantial number of English country houses were built. The large number of new titles granted or, more accurately, sold by James I early in the seventeenth century contributed to this period of extravagant building styles. Aston Hall was one of the largest country houses built during this period in Warwickshire, and a demonstration of the Holte family's success.

Building commenced in 1618; the house was occupied in 1631 and Aston Hall completed in 1635. Good-quality building materials and design were used throughout. For example, instead of rubble foundations as was common at that time, the Hall sits on iron slag, most likely from a furnace at Aston. Bricks for the Hall were manufactured in temporary brick kilns, set up in the Park. Most houses of this period in the area were timber-framed and the materials used for Aston Hall have contributed to its longevity.

James Watt Jnr.

In 1817 the Aston Hall estate was divided by Act of Parliament and the Hall, with some of the Park, was sold. From 1818 James Watt Jnr. rented Aston Hall. He ran the Soho Manufactory and Foundry

▶

The Long Gallery, Aston Hall, is 136 feet long and shows fine original decoration. Little has changed since pre-Victorian times.

◀

Aston Hall is a Jacobean country house. The Park is bordered by Aston Villa football ground on one side and the busy A38(M) on the other.

The kitchen at Aston Hall was added in the mid-18th century. James Watt Jnr. installed a patent steam kitchen range.

with Matthew Robinson Boulton, son of the famous Birmingham industrialist, Matthew Boulton. Aston Hall was the ideal home for Watt. It was close to Soho, appealed to his interest in antiquity and provided a very prestigious place to entertain guests. Indeed, in 1830 Princess Victoria dined at Aston Hall after a tour of the Soho factories. As a tenant, Watt made few structural changes, though he did install modern devices such as a steam kitchen range and hot-air heating.

Corporate Events

In 1848, after James Watt Jnr.'s death, Aston Hall was left empty and in 1850 it was offered for sale to the Corporation of Birmingham. However, negotiations broke down and a group of country gentlemen and artisans formed The Aston Hall and Park Company with the intention of purchasing it. Queen Victoria helped by returning to open the house and an exhibition of Birmingham industrial products on 15 June 1858. Literary dinners and 'old-time Christmas revels' were held to try and raise the additional funds for the purchase; the park was even hired out for corporate celebrations. It was at one such event that Selena Powell, an acrobat known as 'The Female Blondin' fell to her death from a tightrope. After this, Queen Victoria wrote to the town council expressing her displeasure that the park was being used for purposes other than healthy exercise and recreation. Even before this episode the Aston Hall and Park Company was in serious financial difficulty. In November 1863 Queen Victoria wrote again suggesting that a town with such wealth should be able to find the funds to purchase Aston Hall for the population. Finally, in 1864 Aston Hall was sold to Birmingham Corporation and the Hall opened to the public.

Aston Hall's architecture is striking. The main doorway bears the Holte coat of arms and an inscription describing the building process. The stylish character of Jacobean architecture is seen in the Long Gallery and other rooms with their original fine plaster ceilings and panelling. The building is now run by Birmingham Museums and Arts and is one of the hidden delights of Birmingham which deserves a much greater number of visitors.

St Philip's Cathedral

The Church of St Philip was designed by Thomas Archer, known as the 'gentleman architect'. Work

St Philip's Anglican Cathedral was designed in the Baroque style by Thomas Archer. The church was consecrated in 1715 and became Birmingham Cathedral in 1905. This photo was taken shortly after major restoration was completed in 1993 (overleaf).

The Burne-Jones windows in St Philip's Cathedral are examples of 19th-century pre-Raphaelite art. Here are windows depicting the Ascension and the Last Judgement (Doom).

View from the St Philip's cupola, 1993.
There are many historical drawings showing a view of Birmingham where St Philip's dominates the skyline. Here the situation is reversed.

◀

commenced in 1709 and the main building completed in 1715. Archer had visited Rome for inspiration and this is reflected in the fine Roman Baroque detail of St Philip's, most particularly seen in the concave-sided tower. The tower and dome were completed later than the church, in 1725. Birmingham was granted city status in 1889 and St Philip's became a Cathedral in 1905.

A noteworthy feature of the interior is the excellent Pre-Raphaelite windows by Burne-Jones. In the 1980s the Cathedral underwent major restoration which was finished in 1993. The weather-vane on the top of the dome incorporates a boar's head of the Gough-Calthorpe family crest. During restoration this was carefully dismantled and regilded with gold leaf.

Above all else St Philip's Cathedral is very welcoming and an ideal place to stop for a period of quiet reflection, right in the heart of the bustling city.

▶

Soho House, Handsworth.
Now run as a museum this was the home of Matthew Boulton from 1766 until his death in 1809. The house overlooked the famous Soho Manufactory which was just a short distance down the hill. Soho House was often a meeting place for the Lunar Society.

Chapter Three

Boulton, Watt and Soho

T he industrial partnership of Matthew Boulton and James Watt played a significant role in Birmingham's development in the eighteenth century. The inventiveness of these industrialists, and their ability to turn ideas into manufactured products, enabled Birmingham to become a world leader in the supply of steam engines. The enterprise of Boulton and Watt was very important to the growth of Birmingham into a world centre for manufacturing in the eighteenth and nineteenth centuries.

Matthew Boulton, the son of a silver stamper and piercer, was born in Snow Hill, Birmingham in 1728. He became a partner in his father's business making Birmingham 'toys', the name given to items such as buckles, buttons and numerous other trinkets. From the outset Matthew wanted to remove the stigma attached to 'Brummagem' ware, by increasing the quality and reputation of Birmingham's products.

Investing on a Large Scale

In 1759 Boulton senior died and Matthew inherited the family business. He had already married Mary Robinson of Lichfield, who had an inheritance of £14,000. Sadly, she died at around the

◀

The statue of Boulton, Watt and Murdock, Broad Street, Birmingham.
(William Bloye, 1956).

same time as Matthew's father. The following year, at the age of thirty-two, he married Mary's sister Anne Robinson who came with an inheritance of a further £14,000. With this considerable financial security Boulton set about investing in manufacturing activities on a large scale and concentrating on good-quality products.

Boulton established the Soho Manufactory on Handsworth Heath, two miles to the north of Birmingham. The site already had a mill for metal processing and Hockley Brook had been diverted to form a millpond. Soho Pool, as the millpond became known, remained for a hundred years, until drained and filled in to make way for a

Sarehole Mill.
Water mills were an important source of power for Birmingham industry. Matthew Boulton had an interest in Sarehole Mill before he built his famous Soho Manufactory at Handsworth. The Mill is open to the public during the summer months.

railway goods yard. The Soho Manufactory opened in 1764 and Boulton employed good-quality workmen. He was prepared to pay top wages to secure the right skills, a policy which attracted workers from all over Europe. High quality in design was equally encouraged. Boulton travelled to view work at the British Museum and also brought back examples of work from his foreign travels and his enthusiasm for good design quickly paid off. He even received loans of works of art from members of the aristocracy, who gave him much encouragement and support in his work. The Soho Manufactory produced Sheffield plate, silver plate and ormolu of the highest quality as well as the more mundane steel 'toys' such as buckles and buttons. The origins of both the Assay Office and the minting of coins in Birmingham emanated from the enterprise of Boulton (see chapter five).

Soho House

In 1761 Boulton purchased a small Georgian house on a hill-top overlooking the Soho Manufactory and this was his home from 1766 until his death in

1809. He greatly extended and redesigned the house and installed such innovations as central heating, a flush toilet and a hot water supply to the bath, all novelties for their day. Soho House, extensively renovated in 1993/4 is now a heritage centre run by Birmingham Museums and Arts.

Power for the World

By 1770 the Soho Manufactory employed 800 workers, but only had two water wheels to power the equipment. Further expansion was severely limited by lack of power, with horses driving the mills at considerable expense whenever Hockley Brook dried up. Boulton had heard of attempts to use steam engine power and tried experiments himself, but nothing came of them. At the same time James Watt was working on new steam engine designs in Scotland. Watt started to call at Soho on the way home to Scotland from visits to London and was impressed with the quality of the work he saw. In 1770 Watt sent his first completed engine to the Soho Manufactory for testing and in 1774 came to work at Soho himself. With the

Birmingham 'toy making' is an ancient craft that continues in the city to this day. Here a promotional badge is seen in two stages of production at the firm of F.C. Parry, Highgate.

▼

skilled Soho workforce, the inventiveness of Watt and the energy of Boulton, the steam engine design was perfected and Watt's earlier patent of 1769 was extended until 1800.

For twenty-five years Boulton and Watt produced most of the world's steam engines - approximately 500 engines in all. In 1778 they negotiated terms for steam-engine installations in Cornish tin mines, based on the amount of money saved compared with the conventional engines. Indeed, it was advances for powering the Cornish mines which alleviated a serious financial situation for the firm. Boulton, with his entrepreneurial flair, seemed largely untroubled by money problems, but Watt did not enjoy the continual financial insecurity.

The Invention of Gas Lighting

William Murdock called at the Soho Manufactory to ask for work. When Boulton heard that Murdock had turned his wooden hat on a home-made lathe, he was impressed and he was engaged the following day. Murdock was a very reliable engineer and spent many years in Cornwall taking charge of steam-engine installation. However, Murdock's greatest achievement was the invention of gas lighting. Following experiments using different types of coal to make gas, Murdock had his own house in Redruth lit by gaslight. He told Watt

▲

The opening of the Soho Foundry.
The celebrations are portrayed in a mural to be found in the old Post Room of the Soho Foundry which is now part of Avery Berkel.

▶

Detail from the Smethwick Engine.
This 1778 Boulton and Watt engine was built to pump water back up the locks at Smethwick. It is now regularly steamed at the Museum of Science and Industry, and is the oldest working steam engine in the world.

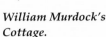

William Murdock's Cottage.
This is believed to have been his residence when he was based at the Soho Foundry.

of his invention and suggested a patent be taken out. However, the firm did not want to take on a new enterprise at that time and Murdock's discovery was not protected. The Soho Manufactory offices were lit by Murdock's invention_and the manufacture of gas-making equipment was added to the list of products. The site of an early gasometer is still to be seen within the Soho Foundry, as is the cottage thought to have been used by Murdock.

Boulton, Watt and Sons

James Watt Jnr. and Matthew Robinson Boulton, sons of the original partners, entered the business in 1794, the firm becoming Boulton, Watt & Sons. Though the steam-engine patent was coming to an end, there was a continuing demand for steam engines and in 1795 they bought land for development next to the canal in Smethwick, where the Soho Foundry was built. The opening of the Soho Foundry in 1796 was marked by a great feast which was attended by the engine-smiths and workers employed in constructing the new works.

Only two steam engines are known to survive from those built during the first phase of production of the Watt steam engine. One is 'Old Bess' an

▶

Traction Engine Rally.
Each May Birmingham holds a steam rally outside the Museum of Science and Industry. The rally includes a parade around St Paul's Square and the church that James Watt and Matthew Boulton both had links with.

experimental engine used at the Soho Manufactory which was built in about 1777, and whose major components are now displayed in the Science Museum in London. The other is the Smethwick Engine of about 1778 which worked until 1892 pumping water back up the locks at Smethwick on the Birmingham Main Line canal. The Smethwick Engine has been renovated and re-erected at the Birmingham Museum of Science and Industry where it is regularly seen working.

After expiry of the steam-engine patent in 1800, the partnership of Boulton and Watt senior was dissolved and the two former partners continued quite separate lives. Watt retired to his home, Heathfield, in Handsworth and continued invent-

ing. He devoted much of his time to constructing an art-carving machine, which could produce replicas of medallions and busts in either enlarged or reduced format. These were his so-called 'parallel eidographs'. He once wrote: 'If I live I hope to be able to produce a reduced copy of Chantrey's bust of myself, fit for a chimney piece as I do not think myself of importance enough to fill up so much of my friends' houses as the original bust does.'

In contrast to James Watt, Matthew Boulton continued to take an active interest in the firm after 1800. He died at the age of eighty-one in August 1809. At his funeral mourners included over 500 workmen from Soho, who were all presented with a commemorative medal. James Watt survived his friend and partner, dying in August 1819 at the age of eighty-three. Boulton and Watt are both buried in Handsworth Parish Church. On the walls of the church are busts of Boulton and Murdock but the chief piece is the sculpture of Watt by Francis Chantrey which was taken as a model for a more recent statue in Chamberlain Square.

Wattilisk
(Vincent Woropay, 1988);
Outside the Queen Elizabeth II Law Courts this sculpture is based on the art-carving machine invention developed by Watt during his retirement.

St Mary's Church, Handsworth.
On the edge of Handsworth Park this was the family church attended by Matthew Boulton, James Watt and William Murdock, who are all buried there.

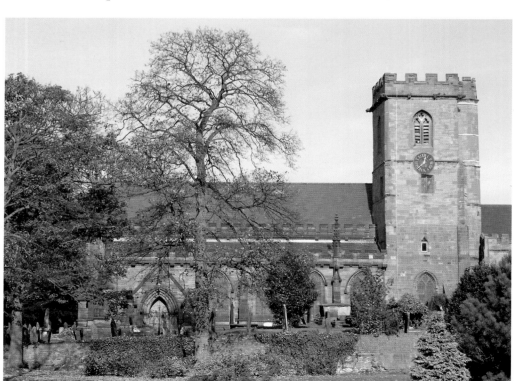

Wattilisk, by Vincent Woropay, placed outside the Queen Elizabeth II Crown Courts just off Corporation Street, is based on the art-carving machine invention. Carved from black Indian granite, *Wattilisk* consists of five portrait heads, which are also based on the Chantrey bust of James Watt in Handsworth Parish Church. Only the uppermost head has the full features of Chantrey's original sculpture. As one moves down, each block becomes less finished, with the lowest one representing an early stage where the sculptor has just begun to determine the shape of the head.

The Lunar Society

Just try to imagine the scale and pace of change in eighteenth-century Birmingham. The coming of the canals, the new manufacturing processes and steam power were just a few of the new developments that those involved in commerce and industry had to keep pace with. A group of prominent progressive figures in and around Birmingham came together and became known as the Lunar Society. Its members, with different areas of expertise were a highly influential philosophical group. They kept no minutes or records of their meetings but much has been learnt about their discussions from the letters of different members.

Meetings of the Lunar Society were held each month at full moon - hence its name - and its two founders were Matthew Boulton and Erasmus Darwin. Also members were James Watt and James Keir, an associate of Boulton who was involved in the chemical industry. Dr William Withering was best known for his discovery of the use of digitalis which was extracted from the foxglove and used in the treatment of heart disease. It is still in use today as the drug digoxin. (At one time Withering was said to be the highest-paid physician outside London.) Other members of the group included Josiah Wedgwood and Joseph Priestley. The total membership of the Lunar Society was around fourteen people, though others were closely associated with the group.

The Lunar Society Room in Soho House includes the original table used for group meetings and a number of products of the Soho Manufactory.

The importance and success of the Lunar Society, due in part to the different professional backgrounds of the membership, is well illustrated by the election of eleven of its members as Fellows of the Royal Society. During its existence from 1766 to 1809 its influence extended far beyond local interests, indeed, well beyond England, and Benjamin Franklin, who became American President, was a close friend of some Lunar Society members. Today a modern-day Lunar Society exists and holds regular meetings to discuss relevant philosophical and historical matters.

Joseph Priestley is now remembered with a statue in Chamberlain Square, where he is depicted in his scientific role as the discoverer of oxygen (1774). However, besides being an eminent scientist of his time and member of the Lunar Society, Priestley was also a nonconformist minister and a radical. He became the minister of the New Meeting House in 1780, the Presbyterian place of worship which was well known for its liberal thinking. Priestley left Birmingham after riots which started on 14 July 1791 and which are now known as the Priestley Riots. To celebrate the second anniversary of the French Revolution, a dinner took place at a hotel in the centre of Birmingham. A mob gathered outside the hotel and violence erupted, with Priestley one of the main targets, even though he did not attend the dinner. The New Meeting House was burnt down and the mob then departed for Priestley's home in Sparkbrook which was destroyed along with his many items of laboratory equipment. Priestley finally left for New York in April 1794, where he spent the rest of his life lecturing and resuming his studies in chemistry.

▶

Winter at Gas Street Basin.

Chapter Four
Canals Rediscovered

Today Birmingham's canals are integral to city-centre redevelopment. Whether it is new offices, a shopping centre, convention centre or pub, a canal frontage is part of the Birmingham architect's brief. Where canals no longer exist they even discuss building them, mock locks and all.

From the end of the Second World War until the 1970s the Birmingham canals were largely forgotten historical backwaters. Access was difficult, they were run down and only real enthusiasts made time to walk along these overgrown and hidden places. Now things are very different. In the late 1970s Birmingham City Council, the Department of the Environment and British Waterways within the Birmingham Inner City Partnership started to implement the city's Canal Improvement Programme. In the early 1980s towpaths were re-paved and access to canals was encouraged by the provision of doorways and new bridges. With the canals increasingly opened up for public use, a fascinating two-hundred-year-old story is now accessible for everyone to discover and enjoy.

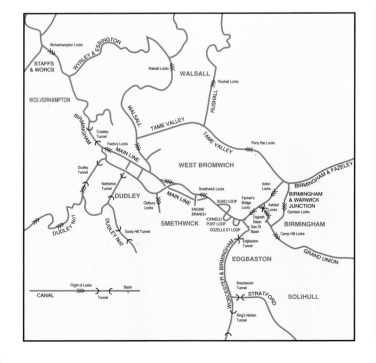

▶

The Guillotine Lock, King's Norton.
At the Junction of the Stratford Canal and the Worcester and Birmingham Canal this lock maintained a 6-inch difference in water level right up to canal nationalisation in 1948.

No Engineering Masterpiece

The original Birmingham canal system was built between the late 1760s and 1830. Canal transport of raw materials from the Black Country, notably coal and iron, was enormously important for Birmingham's industrial expansion. Work on the first canal between the Wednesbury coalfield and Birmingham town centre began in February 1768. The canal was surveyed by the great canal builder James Brindley, whose name now graces a pub in Gas Street Basin. This first section of canal was opened in November 1769. The arrival of Wednesbury coal in Birmingham had a dramatic effect, reducing coal prices by about 50 per cent in the town.

The canal between Birmingham and Wolverhampton was built by the Birmingham Canal Navigations Company (BCN) and was completed in September 1772. The original canal was not a civil engineering masterpiece, essentially following the contours of the land and winding in great loops to avoid expensive earth working. Though bringing great prosperity to Birmingham the canal was soon under pressure from the very large number of people trying to use it. Critics suggested that the excessive length of the Canal had more to do with the fact that transport charges

Curzon Street Railway Bridge, Christmas Eve 1992.
There are still many solitary places on the inner-city canals. The Digbeth Branch is well worth exploring before these secret places become more than just a developer's dream.

▶

Icknield Port Loop.
A cruise on the canal soon gives a different perspective of the city.

▼

◀

were based on 'cost per ton carried per mile' than anything else. The BCN Company was determined to control as much canal trade as possible. The shareholders were Birmingham industrialists and appeared to have two primary aims: to maximise profits from transportation on their canal and to ensure that the price of coal for use in their Birmingham factories was kept as low as possible. The BCN was a highly profitable concern declaring annual dividends as high as 70 per cent and by 1845 the original £140 shares were worth over £3,000.

Bars to Travel

The BCN soon extended its canal system with the Birmingham and Fazeley Canal going east and allowing connections with canal routes to London. Naturally enough, when an alternative route

▶

*The James Brindley is a
popular pub at
Gas Street Basin.*

South, the Worcester and Birmingham Canal, was proposed in 1789 the BCN fought it hard. However, a Parliamentary act for this navigation was finally passed in 1791. In Birmingham the Worcester and Birmingham Canal terminated alongside the BCN canal to form Gas Street Basin, but the BCN Company insisted on a seven-foot-wide area of solid ground between the two canals. It was claimed that this was to prevent the Worcester canal from using up Birmingham's water. In reality the bar was a means of making it uneconomic to use the Worcester and Birmingham Canal to travel south, with the excessive transfer tolls and cranage levied by BCN. The Worcester and Birmingham Canal opened in October 1795 but, not surprisingly, the Company was beset by financial problems and the route to Worcester was not completed until 1815. The Worcester Bar in Gas Street Basin was a source of continual friction between the two canal companies. Eventually in July 1815 the stop lock was opened, but the BCN still continued to levy unreasonable tolls for many years. The stop lock and Worcester Bar can still be seen in Gas Street Basin, with the bar forming the path across the basin.

Granville Street Wharf.
Just round the corner from the ICC and Gas Street Basin life goes on much as it always has.

There are other examples of physical bars between canals owned by different companies. In Digbeth the Warwick Bar prevented unhindered crossing between the BCN Digbeth Branch to the Warwick and Birmingham Canal, which was later to become part of the Grand Union Canal. At King's Norton there is an unusual guillotine lock at the junction of the Stratford Canal and the Birmingham and Worcester Canal. This maintained a six-inch difference in water level between these two canals right up until canal nationalisation in 1948.

A Crooked Ditch

By the early 1820s the canal from Birmingham to the Black Country was suffering from acute congestion. Proposals for railways in Birmingham finally put pressure on the BCN Company to improve the canal through the Black Country to

▲

Old Turn Junction.
A view from the canal can add some life to the somewhat functional architecture of the National Indoor Arena.

Wolverhampton. Thomas Telford was invited to survey the existing canal and was clearly unimpressed, commenting:

> *I found adjacent to this great and flourishing town a canal little better than a crooked ditch, with scarcely the appearance of a hauling path, the horses frequently sliding and staggering in the water, the hauling lines sweeping the gravel into the canal, and the entanglement at the meeting of boats incessant; while at the locks at each end of the short summit crowds of boatmen were always quarrelling or offering premiums for a preference of passage.*

Telford's remedies included widening the Main Line, straightening the canal and building a new reservoir at Edgbaston to improve water provision. His plan included eight miles of new canal, completed in 1827, which reduced the journey between Birmingham and Wolverhampton by seven miles. However, despite the shorter distance, the BCN Company, in traditional style, continued to levy tolls based on the mileage of the old route.

Edgbaston Reservoir.
A good supply of water is critical to a successful canal system. In the 1820s Thomas Telford straightened the canal to Wolverhampton and this new reservoir was built at Edgbaston.

▼

Railway and Canal Side by Side

Eventually the railways led to the decline of canal transportation, but for many years canal and railway flourished side by side. Between 1848 and 1898 the tonnage of goods carried on the canals nearly doubled, showing the benefit of both improving the canal system and integrating it with the newer railways.

In the twentieth century older industries which were based alongside the canal system, started to disappear. At the same time the increase in road and rail transportation of raw products and finished goods accelerated the decline in the Birmingham canal system. After the Second World War the future of the canals looked grim. Movement of goods onto the growing motorway network of the 1960s finally meant the end of commercial traffic on the Birmingham canal system. The British Transport Commission and local authorities could see no use for the canals and only the cost of filling them in saved the present 145 miles of Birmingham and Black Country canals.

Dredging the Main Line.
Work on the towpaths and locks has done much to improve the canals while Project Aquarius removed 40,000 cubic yards of polluted industrial silt from ten miles of city canal. The water quality has improved and fishermen now help to monitor the effects on fish stocks.
▼

Gradually canal enthusiasts have increased in number and in the 1970s and 1980s the leisure use of canals rose very fast around the country. Although the Birmingham canals were not then a natural holiday centre because of their rather barren surroundings, this has now changed. An increased interest in industrial heritage has helped, as has the major investment in the canal system and the surrounding environment, including towpath and lock reconstruction, dredging, provision of new moorings, and improved public access.

New Uses for Old Waterways

With their renewed economic and leisure use, canals have become central to many new developments in Birmingham. It is now possible to walk along newly renovated towpaths on all the Birmingham city-centre canals. Many people are taking advantage of the new environment in all sorts of ways. The towpath from Birmingham to Wolverhampton has been improved with cyclists particularly in mind; landscaping has been undertaken on many parts of the canal; fishing is now possible with an increasing chance of success and these two-hundred-year canal corridors provide a haven for wildlife of all descriptions.

The Soho Loop, close to City Hospital, has a keen angling club that meets on Sunday mornings. Fish such as roach and gudgeon are common catches. At the end of Project Aquarius 1,500 roach and 1,000 ghost carp, a cross between a regular carp and koi carp, were released into the canal.

55

Thomas the Tank Engine Day at Birmingham Railway Museum is a great day out. It was the coming of the railways and later the roads, that led to the gradual decline of commercial traffic on the canals.

▶

The legacy of years of industrial activity beside the canals has left a great quantity of polluted silt, which still hinders ecological diversification of the canals. In 1993/94, with Project Aquarius, the city's canals were dredged to clear out some of this polluted silt in an attempt to improve the water quality.

Narrowboats are used as permanent homes in the city, the most well known being those of the people who still manage to live in Gas Street Basin. However, by 1993 their number had reduced to just nine people, largely owing to pressures created by canalside development. Indeed by early 1994 many of these 'high profile' canal dwellers had moved round the corner to Cambrian Wharf leaving very few long-term inhabitants in Gas Street Basin. However, if you know where to look, you will find narrowboats moored on old arms of the canal system, no longer used by industry, in a number of places close to the city centre. About

Spaghetti Junction is a suitable symbol of the movement of transportation from rail to road

fifty people are thought to be presently living on narrowboats in Birmingham itself with more in the surrounding areas.

New Designs for Old Waterways

Narrowboats are being built at several boatyards on the canal system, not far from Birmingham, and these are for both purchase and hire use. The last boats constructed in Birmingham itself were at a yard at Sherborne Street Wharf which closed at the end of 1993. We can only hope that it will not be too long before narrowboats are once again built in Birmingham.

Research on a new environmentally friendly 'Eco' hull was undertaken for British Waterways at Glasgow University and a prototype boat built in 1991. Below the water line the Eco hull has a semi-cylindrical bow-shape, similar to that of a modern ship. The design was apparently influenced by the rounded snouts of whales. The new hull is intended to reduce the bow and pressure waves on the canal banks and bottom, lessening damage to the canal as the narrowboat passes through.

Although carriage of goods on Birmingham canals has ceased, commercial traffic in the form of business seminars and tourist trips is now an everyday sight. Such trips get off to a good start with a safety announcement, which includes the

▲

Al Harris of Alvechurch Boat Centre handing John Townsend the keys to Gazebo. This was the 11th Eco hull built by Alvechurch Boat Centre. Gazebo is 67 feet long and is powered by a 1,400 cc Lister engine. Note the small bow wave as the boat travels along at 4 miles an hour.

encouraging statement; 'Don't worry, if the boat sinks just stand up and walk to the bank!'

Interest in the history of the canals and their recreational use is growing all the time. There are considerable lengths of canal still to be re-developed, for example in Digbeth, with interesting Victorian buildings all around. Coming across the Warwick Bar or Digbeth Canal Basin, seeing the Gun Barrel Proof House from the canal or experiencing a Christmas Eve sunset reflected on the walls of Curzon Street railway bridge can make for an unforgettable walk. It is as you explore these more secret parts of the Birmingham canal system, that you appreciate the enormous potential the canals still offer for commercial and leisure development within the city.

▲

The National Sealife Centre is part of the Brindleyplace development and attracts huge numbers of visitors to the city centre canalside. The building was designed by Sir Norman Foster and Partners and opened in June 1996.

▶

The Birmingham Assay Office, Newhall Street, where it has been since 1877. It was first established in 1773 in rented rooms above the King's Head, New Street.

Chapter Five

The Jewellery Quarter

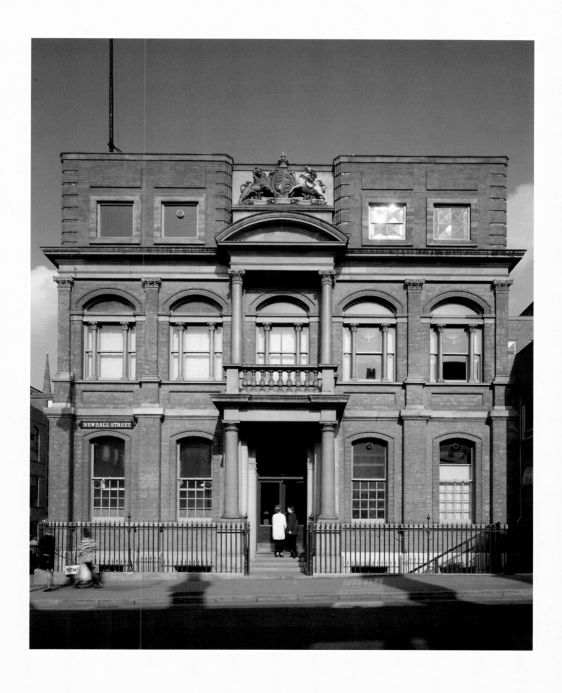

The Birmingham Jewellery Quarter is a ten-minute walk from the city centre and a fascinating area to visit and explore. It is a workplace, a rich source of industrial architecture and increasingly, an important centre for tourism. The jewellery industry has been established in Birmingham for around 200 years and almost from the start it has been concentrated in this one district.

Joseph Chamberlain, a great supporter of the jewellery industry, is closely associated with the Jewellery Quarter, which he represented as MP for many years. The Chamberlain Clock right in the centre of the Jewellery Quarter marks this association. Unveiled in 1904 by Mr and Mrs Chamberlain, this well-known landmark has been renovated and is a natural focus for the Quarter.

In the nineteenth century, the Jewellery Quarter became a densely developed part of Birmingham. The industry relies on a marked division of labour with a multitude of specialist skills requiring the transfer of part-finished items between different craftsmen's workshops. The original development began when the Colmore family sold plots of land for building in the eighteenth century - Ann Colmore granted leases on parts of her estate from 1746 and Birmingham 'toy' makers moved into many of the houses with the area soon becoming a centre for this occupation. Later, in the mid-nineteenth century Colonel Vyse released land in a similar way. A large part of the Vyse Estate of villa-style residential housing was converted to commercial use and much of this can still be seen in the Quarter today. As the jewellery trade expanded, houses on these two estates were converted into multi-occupied business premises. These conversions often included the building of 'shopping' in the back yards and extensions at the front on upper levels - many of them still to be found in the Quarter.

▶

The Chamberlain Clock.
This commemorates the connection between the Jewellery Quarter and Joseph Chamberlain, who represented the area as an MP. The clock was purchased by public subscription to mark the efforts of Chamberlain in his services to the Empire in South Africa. The white building behind is the Big Peg.

The jewellery industry has always attracted small business enterprise, because so little capital investment was required for many of the crafts. An artisan needed a bench, or 'peg' as it was termed, and a few hand tools. Many different factors enabled the Birmingham Jewellery Quarter industries to develop and survive the periods of recession. The continued presence of the Birmingham Assay Office, local engineering and tool-making expertise, the existence of precious-metal dealers and a ready gas supply, have all been important in the industry's survival.

The Assay Office

The Birmingham Assay Office first opened in 1773 in rented rooms above the King's Head public house in New Street and its existence was largely due to the petitioning of Parliament by Matthew Boulton. At that time his Soho Manufactory was starting to produce good-quality silverware but the goods had to be sent to the Chester Assay Office for hallmarking. This was both costly and inconvenient and meant that Birmingham products were not getting full recognition. The silver makers of both Birmingham and Sheffield petitioned Parliament together for their own Assay Offices. Despite opposition from London craftsman, Boulton, who by then had considerable influence, managed to get the Act passed. Appropriately, it was items from the Soho Manufactory which were the first products to be handled by the new Assay Office.

Today the Birmingham Assay Office is in Newhall Street, opposite the Museum of Science and Industry. The present building dates from 1877 and on one wall, to the right of the main entrance, is the anchor mark, the Birmingham Assay Office Town Mark. It is thought that it was derived from the name of the Crown and Anchor Inn where much of the committee work was done in promoting the bill in Parliament. When Sheffield and Birmingham gained approval for their respective Assay Offices the story goes that the Town Marks were decided on the toss of a coin, Birmingham ending up with an anchor and Sheffield a crown.

Much of the growth of the Jewellery Quarter has been based on individual craftsmen who often worked as outworkers for larger traders. However,

◄

Anchor Town Mark.
On the side of the Assay Office is the anchor which forms part of the hallmark on items assayed by the Birmingham office. There are four assay offices in Britain, Sheffield, London and Edinburgh being the others.

▲

The Birmingham Mint was started by Ralph Heaton and initially used equipment from the Soho Manufactory. The present building dates from 1861.

there have also been much bigger companies specialising in different areas of the jewellery trade. In particular the process of electroplating was perfected in the Quarter and the firm of Elkington had a large factory on Newhall Street, now the home of the Birmingham Museum of Science and Industry.

The Birmingham Mint

Another large-scale undertaking in the Jewellery Quarter has been the minting of coins and tokens. This activity was pioneered at the Soho Manufactory, by Matthew Boulton, where steam driven machines were used to produce coins for the reign of George III. The Soho coins were of a much better quality than those produced previously and did much to stop the output of forgeries, production of which had probably also been centred in Birmingham! Following this success, Boulton was contracted to install equipment at the

Royal Mint, which was used for the next seventy years.

The Birmingham Mint itself was established by Ralph Heaton who had expertise in the brass industry and 'toy' making, both important skills for minting coinage. He bought the Soho Manufactory minting equipment at auction and started to make coins for the home market and the colonies. The Mint moved to its present site in Icknield Street in 1860 and installed new machinery in the 1870s, which provided greater capacity than the Royal Mint in London. Indeed the Birmingham Mint was sub-contracted to do much of the Royal Mint's work, while they sorted out machinery problems in London. The size of the operation is illustrated by orders from Russia during 1896-98 which amounted to annual production of 110 million coins. Today, now part of IMI plc, the IMI Birmingham Mint produces coins and blanks for many countries and medals and tokens for a wide range of markets. Having the foresight to re-equip with modern machinery at the right time has ensured the continued existence of the Mint. Indeed, it now has one of the world's foremost coin blank-plating facilities. Today, the IMI Birmingham Mint has the capacity for every part of coin production - initial casting of alloys is followed by milling, rolling and annealing after which blanks are cleaned and struck.

The Only Remaining Georgian Square

St Paul's Square in the Jewellery Quarter, is the one remaining Georgian square in Birmingham. In the centre of the Square is St Paul's Church. Designed by the architect Roger Eykyn, it dates from 1779 and was built on land donated by Charles Colmore, who also gave £1,000 towards the cost of building. Further money for building the church was raised by selling freeholds for pew seats at £5 each. These were later re-sold and even bequeathed, and it took a hundred years for this seating to be released for general use. Matthew

Painted Window, St Paul's Church
(Eginton, 1791).
Francis Eginton initially worked with Boulton at the Soho Manufactory. This fine painted window depicts the conversion of St Paul and is from the study of a painting by the American artist Benjamin West.

▼

Boulton and James Watt both had pews, though their family church was St Mary's, Handsworth. The fine painted east window was produced by Francis Eginton, who originally worked with Boulton at the Soho Manufactory before setting up his own workshops.

The houses of the square were originally built for residential use, but as the Jewellery Quarter expanded, this desirable district was slowly surrounded by factories, with many buildings in the square also being turned over to manufacturing. Recently the square became a conservation area and restoration of the old Georgian buildings and the church has been undertaken; many of the properties have been redeveloped yet again, this time for office use.

Architectural Jewels

There is a wealth of interesting Victorian architecture to see in the Jewellery Quarter. The Argent Centre, on Frederick Street, one of the most attractive buildings in the Quarter, was constructed in 1863 for W. E. Wiley, a manufacturer of gold pens

St Paul's Church was completed in 1779 and has been extensively renovated in the last few years. The church is often used for staging musical events, just as it was in the 18th century.

▶

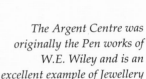

The Argent Centre was originally the Pen works of W.E. Wiley and is an excellent example of Jewellery Quarter architecture. It is now sub-divided into small business premises.

▼

and pencils, and is built in the Renaissance style. The architect used hollow bricks and wrought iron ties in the construction, claiming that these doubled the weight-bearing capacity of the floors and reduced the fire risk. The factory employed 250 workers in pen production and a further thirty-five used the excess steam from the factory to operate a Turkish bath. The building has been refurbished and is one of a number of centres providing small units for industrial and commercial use.

One of the best examples of the many redevelopments of Victorian buildings for modern use is the Jewellery Quarter Business Centre in Spencer Street which was undertaken by the Duchy of Cornwall and has been a focus for HRH the Prince of Wales's ideas on the regeneration of inner city areas. The development provides modern office and industrial premises for a wide range of different businesses. The £2.5 million development

▲

Pen Nib Works.
There is still just about evidence of a surviving Birmingham pen industry, which used to dominate the world in the 19th century.

▶

The gates to the Jewellery Quarter Business Centre (Michael Johnson, 1991). This redevelopment, by the Duchy of Cornwall, is closely linked with Prince Charles.

includes an unusual sculpture in the form of the entrance gates to the reception area. These are constructed from stainless steel and brass, which relate to the traditional silver and gold of the jewellery industry; cut glass 'jewels' are incorporated in the design which is meant to represent the 'tree of life'.

The former Hockley Centre is a large development, which was the result of 1960s ideas to try to redevelop the Jewellery Quarter. At that time many premises were in a very poor state of repair. It was thought that replacing them with a large modern building, sub-divided into units would encourage the interrelationships of craftsmen. In practice rents were too high and when the units were first let in 1971 they took eighteen months to occupy fully. The idea has not been repeated and emphasis has shifted to renovation and upgrading of existing buildings. The Hockley Centre, now renamed the 'Big Peg', has itself undergone renovation and seems to be establishing a clearer identity within the Quarter.

Emphasis on Education

The Jewellery Quarter is still a major centre for production of jewellery, medals, badges and associated crafts. A School of Jewellery opened in 1890 and is still located in the Quarter, now as part of the University of Central England and has recently undergone redevelopment. An emphasis on education must be one of the reasons for the survival of the industry in the Quarter. Employment in the Birmingham jewellery industry has always been relatively modest with a peak of perhaps 40,000 in 1913 which represented about 7 per cent of total employment in the city. In 1984 the industry was estimated to be employing about 5,000 workers. The continued need for a close-knit industrial community is shown by the high failure rate of those firms which decide to move away from the Quarter. The many newly renovated units in the Quarter offer excellent opportunities for

Naughty Fox and Red Hen. This unusual modern jewellery is by local designer Lyn Antley. In silver and brass it is an earring stand containing a silver fox pin-brooch and silver bird earrings.

▼

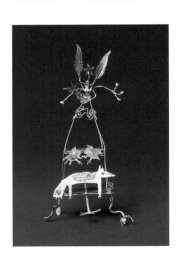

small businesses to become established, and commercial accommodation has comparatively low rents and is very convenient for the city centre.

A Tourist Centre

What was once an area known only to those who had business in the Quarter, has more recently become a busy tourist centre. This has led to a large number of retail outlets opening and selling jewellery at bargain prices and today the number of individual craftsmen in the Jewellery Quarter appears to be increasing once again. Their work is not always easy to find, though it is well worth taking the time to seek them out among the larger discount jewellery outlets.

The Jewellery Quarter now has a Discovery Centre at the premises of the former firm of Smith and Pepper, a traditional Jewellery Quarter business which closed in 1981. The premises were bought

and preserved as they had been left, by Birmingham Museums and Arts. This old works is now an award-winning museum which tells the fascinating story of the Quarter. However, this is much more than a museum, for present-day Jewellery Quarter workers can be seen demonstrating their skills at the centre, which also retails an interesting range of work from the craftsmen in the Quarter.

Birmingham Gun Quarter

Gun-making also involves the interaction of a number of specialised craftsmen. In Birmingham the production of hand-made guns became centred on an area close to St Chad's Cathedral. By the end of the seventeenth century Birmingham was supplying 200 muskets a month to the Government and during the Napoleonic Wars three million gun barrels were made in the town. Birmingham supplied almost every firearm in the country until the 1880s when Belgian imports began to encroach and the ordinance factory at Enfield was established. Guns were tested at the Proof House, which was built in 1813, and is still to be found in Banbury Street backing on to Digbeth Canal Basin.

In 1861 the Birmingham Small Arms (BSA) factory opened in Small Heath and large-scale Birmingham gun-making moved away from small workshop production. However, the craft of hand-made specialist gun-making has continued,

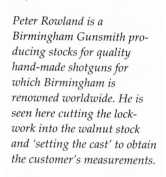

Peter Rowland is a Birmingham Gunsmith producing stocks for quality hand-made shotguns for which Birmingham is renowned worldwide. He is seen here cutting the lockwork into the walnut stock and 'setting the cast' to obtain the customer's measurements.

though the inner ring road, built in the 1960s, swept through and destroyed the heart of the Gun Quarter. However, there are visible signs that the industry continues and sporting guns made in Birmingham still have an excellent reputation.

▶

Ladypool Junior and Infant School
(Martin and Chamberlain).
This impressive building is just one of many such school buildings that can still be seen around the city. Note the ventilation shaft incorporated into the Gothic design.

Chapter Six

Ideals in Terracotta

Terracotta façades became one of the great architectural symbols of the late nineteenth century, and the drive to improve the fabric and infrastructure of Birmingham. Terracotta was a hard-wearing building material, well suited to industrial, nineteenth-century Birmingham life; it allowed designers to express new ideals and commercial and industrial success for the many new buildings of the period.

Terracotta was used for linings both outside and inside buildings. These decoratively moulded clay blocks offered distinctive bright colours, usually red or buff, good resistance to corrosion from smoke and soot, and sharpness of intricate detail that could not be achieved using carved stonework. Terracotta production was centred on Midland towns around Birmingham. However, many of the most distinctive red façades were manufactured at Ruabon, North Wales, known as 'terracottopolis', where the plentiful clay supplies were a by-product of mining.

Moulded terracotta linings began to be used in façades with carved stone. A good example of this is Oozells Street School on Broad Street, which was built in 1878 and now forms part of the Brindleyplace development. Tiled pavements, a forerunner of terracotta, can be seen in the 1840 work by Minton in St Chad's Cathedral.

St Chad's Cathedral was designed by the leading architect of the Gothic revival, A.W. N. Pugin (1840). It pre-dates the use of terracotta.

▶

Early tiled pavements by Minton dating from the 1840s can be seen in St Chad's Roman Catholic Cathedral. They are an example of the collaboration between Minton and A.W.N. Pugin.

▼

Architecture to Express Ideals

If terracotta was the physical way of expressing new ideals then Joseph Chamberlain was the man who helped make it all happen. Like a number of other influential Birmingham citizens, Chamberlain was not Birmingham born, but a Londoner who came to Birmingham in 1854 to help in the screw-making factory of his uncle, J.S. Nettlefold. The firm wanted to introduce new American equipment to improve production and he required additional capital for his venture. He approached Chamberlain senior for financial help and his son,

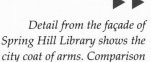

Statue to George Dawson
(T. Woolner, 1885).
George Dawson (1821-1876)
was one of a group of free-
church radical ministers who
preached the Civic Gospel
and Joseph Chamberlain was
among his congregation.

▶▶

Detail from the façade of
Spring Hill Library shows the
city coat of arms. Comparison
with today's version in
Victoria Square shows some
interesting differences.

Joseph Chamberlain, arrived in Birmingham as part of the deal.

The town that Chamberlain came to work in was clearly suffering as a result of enormous industrial expansion. By the mid-nineteenth century Birmingham had become the major hardware manufacturing centre of the world. The largely uncontrolled industrial growth and urban expansion had brought great social and economic problems. People worked long hours in unhealthy and dangerous conditions, returning home to poor-quality housing, which lacked basic amenities such as a clean water supply and sewage disposal.

In 1832 the Reform Act had given Birmingham two Members of Parliament. In 1851 the Improvement Act established a system for local government, giving the Town Council control of public buildings, markets, roads, lighting and sewerage. However, when Chamberlain first arrived few improvements had actually been made. The town still had 50,000 back-to-back houses, lacked proper sewage disposal and refuse collection and relied on water from polluted wells. It is not surprising that in inner-city districts, 20 per cent of children died before they were old enough to walk.

The Nettlefold firm began to make large profits based on new manufacturing processes and the company came to dominate the wood screw market. This success enabled Chamberlain to spend time considering the problems of the living and working conditions around him in Birmingham. He was influenced by the Lancashire radical John Bright, who became a Member of Parliament for Birmingham in 1857. The teachings of preachers such as George Dawson were also highly influential in the development of ideas that became known as the 'Civic Gospel' and which led to a period of unparalleled change in the town.

Spring Hill Library.
This is an excellent example of graceful Gothic design and includes intricate terracotta detail. (Martin and Chamberlain, 1893)

Radical Change Soundly Financed

Chamberlain was particularly interested in improvements to education. In 1869, he became a Town Councillor for St Paul's ward in the Jewellery Quarter, becoming a member of the Birmingham School Board in 1870 and Mayor of Birmingham in 1873. In a speech as Mayor, he set out his aims for a radical programme of improvements and he promised that the town 'shall not, with God's help, know itself!'.

Purchase of the two gas companies and the waterworks by the Council helped finance municipal development. These utilities were modernised and expanded under Council control, producing substantial profits, which could be used to fund other projects. Chamberlain appointed a medical officer and set up a Drainage Board to look at the disposal of sewage and refuse; public parks were opened and public transport started. The grandest scheme of Chamberlain's Council, known as the Improvement Scheme, involved the demolition of ninety acres of slums in the town centre together with the development of Corporation Street. Chamberlain was as astute in municipal finances

Moseley Road Baths and Library.
Not every building of this period was designed by Martin and Chamberlain. The library was by architects Cossins and Peacock (1896) and the baths in yellow-brown terracotta by William Hale (1907).

Highbury, the home of Joseph Chamberlain, designed by John H. Chamberlain (no relation) and completed in 1880, uses a mixture of stone and plaster as well as terracotta. John H. Chamberlain was a follower of Ruskin and his designs were richly decorated. Highbury is now owned by Birmingham City Council and is opened to the public several times a year.

▼

The hall at Highbury is a central feature of the house and is overlooked on all sides by the first floor balcony.
▶

as he had been in manufacturing and because many of the developments he initiated were funded by the municipal gas company's profits, the increases in rates were never as high as predicted by his political opponents. Payments on the leases on the newly constructed Corporation Street shops and offices soon recovered the costs for that scheme.

When after three years as Mayor, Chamberlain was elected a Member of Parliament he took a London residence near Hyde Park and also had a house built in Birmingham, named Highbury after his childhood home in London. John H. Chamberlain, (no relation to Joseph Chamberlain) was responsible for the design of Highbury. With his partner William Martin, John H. Chamberlain was at the forefront of new building design in Birmingham during the 'municipal revolution'.

Schools to Look Up to

With the Education Act of 1870 many schools and educational institutions were built and these new schools contrasted with the densely packed, poor-quality dwellings surrounding them. During this period the firm of Martin and Chamberlain were the architects responsible for forty-one board schools up to 1898, though John H. Chamberlain

This was King Edward VI Grammar School, Camp Hill (Martin and Chamberlain, 1893) until 1958 when the school moved to Vicarage Road, King's Heath. The building was renovated in 1993.

himself died in 1883 at the age of fifty-two. They favoured the Gothic style and used deep red brick and terracotta, with towers that often rose to a considerable height. This architectural partnership almost had a monopoly on the design of public buildings in Birmingham such as free libraries, public baths, asylums and water-pumping stations. Many of these buildings are still in excellent condition. Spring Hill Library has a large tower and the terracotta detail includes the city coat of arms. This is now beside a busy round-about, or 'island' as they are called in Birmingham. Free libraries first came to Birmingham in 1861 and by 1911 there were eleven in the city.

Victoria Law Courts

Corporation Street was the most dramatic demon-stration of the Civic Gospel. Although much has gone, the Aston end still has a striking group of terracotta decorated buildings. These include the Victoria Law Courts (1887-91), the General Hospital (1892-7), now to be the Children's Hospital, and the Methodist Central Hall (1899-1903). The Victoria Law Courts, originally intended for the site of the Council House exten-sion, ended up at the top of Corporation Street. The building is a fine example of the use of terracotta, the typical red on the outside contrast-ing with the yellow-brown in the great hall inside. Terracotta is much more extensively used in this building than anywhere previously.

Terracotta to Drink in

Richly decorated terracotta helped to impress local building officials and licensing justices. The 1890s saw a major redevelopment and expansion of public houses in Birmingham. Between 1889 and 1914 terracotta was used on about twenty-six Birmingham pubs which were mainly the work of the architects James and Lister Lea and also William Jenkins, with the Hathern Station Brick and Terracotta Company. Much of the detail on the

◄

The Victoria Law Courts (Aston Webb and Ingress Bell, 1887-91), at the end of Corporation Street, display intricate use of terracotta in a mixture of architectural styles.

façades of these pubs reflects the prolific artistic expression of the Hathern staff. The Red Lion in Soho Road, Handsworth, a good example of their designs, was built for the Holt Brewery Company and was more ambitious than many of the other James and Lister Lea pubs. It has deep red terracotta on the ground floor and buff terracotta above. With its Jacobean-style detail and heraldic lions, it looks as good as new today right in the centre of Handsworth.

Changing Fashions

Gradually fashions changed in the early twentieth century and terracotta gave way to faience, a glazed ceramic material which was used on a large

The Red Palace is an imposing red brick and terracotta building, built in 1896, which served as a memorial to Lord Roberts of Kandahar, Commander in Chief of the British Empire.

▶

The Red Lion Public House, Soho Road, Handsworth, was designed in 1902 by James and Lister Lea, who were responsible for many of the terracotta pubs in Birmingham.

▼

The Marlborough now sits alone in Anderton Road, Sparkbrook (William Jenkins, 1900). Jenkins was already in his sixties when the 1890s pub building boom arrived.

◀

number of Birmingham buildings up to the Second World War.

Today there is increasing interest in Victorian terracotta architecture and there is an abundance of examples in Birmingham city centre and in the suburbs.

▶

Birdlife
(Ron Haselden, 1991).
The glass for this sculpture was blown by Laszlo Gregor in the Jewellery Quarter.

Chapter Seven

Art on the Streets

Public art is not a new concept in Birmingham and there are many examples to see in the city dating from Victorian times. Even older is the bronze statue of Lord Nelson by Richard Westmacott in the Bull Ring, one of the earliest monuments to Nelson in Britain (1809).

However, as Birmingham has undergone redevelopment a great deal of attention has recently been given to public art. This now requires proper examination. The concept of setting aside a proportion of the capital costs of a building

Lord Nelson Statue
(Richard Westmacott, 1809)
An old public statue in
the Bull Ring.
▼

programme to help fund public art projects has provided many works of art. Birmingham has been at the forefront of the 'one per cent for art' initiative, applying it during the building of the International Convention Centre and Centenary Square. Following this success, public art has been integrated into the redevelopment of Victoria Square. It is also seen on other projects such as the Heartlands development, to the east of the city centre.

Centenary Square

Centenary Square was designed by artists Tess Jaray and Tom Lomax in conjunction with City Council Architects and was completed in 1991. Paving designs and other features such as seating, lighting, railings and plants have all been integrated into the design for the Square.

Speaking of her Centenary Square work Tess Jaray said:

> *I discovered that the differences between conceiving a painting and conceiving an idea for an actual site are not as great as they might first appear. Therefore, the proposal for Centenary Square was always seen as a total concept, as a painting must be. Every aspect, each element, must function in its own right, for its own purpose, but still be part of the whole.*

Within this integrated concept of a square there are also a number of more formal works of art. Each is quite different, but one thing they have in common is the feel of a city that is both prepared to take stock of its past and is looking forward to the future in a very positive way.

Don't Forget the Past

There are several works of art in Centenary Square which have been around for many years. Round the Hall of Memory (1923-4) are four sculptures in bronze by Albert Toft. Across Broad Street, outside the Registry Office, is a sculpture by William Bloye erected in 1956. This is a larger-than-life represen-

▶

New Year Fireworks in Centenary Square. The first New Year Party in Centenary Square marked the start of 1992 and the Sounds Like Birmingham year of music. An estimated 50,000 people enjoyed the spectacle.
(overleaf)

tation of the famous eighteenth-century Birmingham industrialists Boulton, Watt and Murdock.

Forward into the Future

A more controversial piece of public art in Centenary Square, is the statue *Forward* by Raymond Mason (1991). Taking its name from the city's motto, *Forward* was cast in resin at the well-known Haligon Studios near Paris. Mason was Birmingham born and worked with Bloye when he was Master of Modelling at Birmingham School of Art. He moved to France in the 1940s and has become internationally known for his large-scale figurative sculptures. For his home city he has represented the onward march of the people of Birmingham. Backed by the power-house of the city's industry the figures grow in size towards the front, where a worker holds up his industrial hand. Included among the figures are the Chamberlains and the Lady of the Arts from the city coat of arms, seen throwing a kiss to the past, while an actress offers a bouquet to the Birmingham Repertory Theatre across the Square.

The *Forward* statue has stimulated a widening public discussion on art in the City of Birmingham and on these grounds alone it must be considered a success, but it has met with a mixed response from the Birmingham public. Perhaps one should remember that when Bloye's statue of Boulton, Watt and Murdock was put up in Broad Street it was described as representing 'Mr Lee and Mr Longland selling a carpet or inspecting a roll of wallpaper', Lee Longlands being an old established department store close by in Broad Street.

Enterprise Cast in Bronze

There are three further contemporary works of art in Centenary Square. Centrally placed is the Tom Lomax water sculpture *The Spirit of Enterprise* (1991) which has three large sand-cast bronze dishes supporting allegories of Commerce, Industry and

Detail from the Forward statue ▶

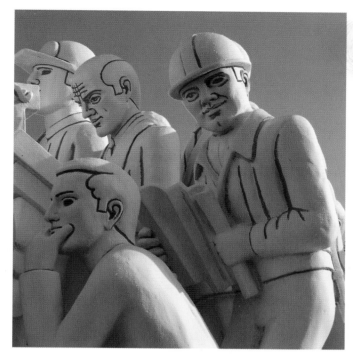

Forward, Centenary Square (Raymond Mason, 1991), is constructed from fibreglass, with resin and polymer paint, and is centrally positioned in Centenary Square.

▲
Spirit of Enterprise
(Tom Lomax, 1991)
Three great bronze dishes
support allegories of
Commerce, Industry and
Enterprise.

▶

The allegories of Commerce
(left) and Industry (right) are
certainly strong images.

Enterprise. Lomax intended the flow of water through the sculpture to indicate the passage of time, with the circles portraying symbols of eternity and the cascade of water down the curved steps helping to integrate the fountain with the surroundings.

Monument to John Baskerville

Outside Baskerville House is David Patten's Portland stone and bronze sculpture *Monument to John Baskerville - Industry and Genius* (1990), which lies close to the site of Easy Hill the residence of John Baskerville. As an influential eighteenth-century Birmingham industrialist Baskerville had two quite different driving forces.

► *Industry and Genius*
(David Patten, 1990)
A representation of the Baskerville type-punches, spells out the title (in reverse) of the first work printed by Baskerville.

He was an entrepreneur, making his fortune from various manufacturing ventures including japanning and papier-mâché production, but he is best remembered for developing a stylish typeface and using it to print classical works on his printing press. The printing side of his business seems to have been only marginally profitable and perhaps he pursued it as much to satisfy an artistic urge. His first book, *The Poems of Virgil*, was produced in 1757 and sold at a guinea.

Although Baskerville was a non-believer he took great pains to publish the Common Prayer Book and the Bible. He became the printer to Cambridge University in December 1758 and completed a magnificent folio Bible in 1763.

Baskerville died on 8 January 1775 at the age of sixty-nine and at his request was buried in a vertical position in his garden. On his monumental urn it read: 'Stranger - beneath this cone, in unconsecrated ground a friend to the liberties of mankind directed his body be inurn'd.'

In the 1820s the site of Easy Hill was transformed into a canal wharf, Baskerville's body was uncovered, found to be in good condition, and was exhibited to the public. A local bookseller stopped this spectacle by secretly transferring the body to the vaults of Christchurch, at the head of New Street. When Christchurch was demolished in 1899 the body was removed to the catacombs of Warstone Lane cemetery where it remains to this day.

Industry and Genius symbolises the type-punch for the Baskerville typeface, spelling out the title of his first book, Virgil, back to front.

The Gods and the Giants

The bronze cloud sculpture on the piazza at the canalside entrance of the International Convention Centre was completed by Coventry-born artist Roderick Tye in 1992. It has been said that the calm

of the exterior of *The Battle of the Gods and Giants* is contrasted by the rough interior. However, speaking of his work Roderick Tye suggests that the piece should be 'free of any particular modern emblematic context'.

Public Art in the International Convention Centre

Inside the ICC there are a number of pieces of public art. *Birdlife* (1991) is a neon sculpture incorporated into the canopy at the front entrance of the ICC. By Ron Haselden, this 'living' multi-coloured neon represents an abstract tree growing up through an aviary. The movement of the sculpture is computer controlled and simulates the migration of birds, perhaps symbolising international travel.

On the canalside of the ICC is a large abstract stained glass design by Alexander Beleschenko (1991). It contains over 50,000 pieces of hand cut and shaped coloured glass and is encased between two sheets of toughened clear glass.

▲
Battle of the Gods & Giants
(Roderick Tye, 1992)
On the canalside entrance to the ICC by the bridge to Brindleyplace.

Birdlife
(Ron Haselden, 1991).
▼

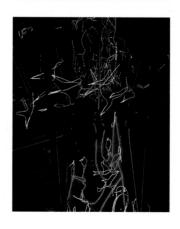

This abstract Stained Glass Window is found above the canalside entrance to the International Convention Centre (Alexander Beleschenko, 1991).

◀

▶

Construction: An Allegory *(Vincent Woropay, 1992). This work looks at different types of construction over the ages. It was appropriately sponsored by Robert M. Douglas Holdings plc, the ICC main building contractors. See also Wattilisk on page 39 by the same artist.*

Just off the ICC mall at the front entrance is *Construction: An Allegory* by Vincent Woropay (1992). This chromium-plated and bronze sculpture considers the history of building techniques. The sculpture contrasts three types of building practices with contemporary building props supporting classical Doric columns, which in their turn support a primitive wooden hut. This piece is by the same sculptor as the superb *Wattilisk* to be found outside the Birmingham New Crown Courts.

Other works of art on display in the ICC include *Symphony Hall Mural*, an oil mural on four floors by Deanna Petherbridge and *The Convention*, a wooden sculpture on the wall on the Symphony Hall side of the Mall by Richard Perry.

Symphony Hall Mural *(Deanna Petherbridge,1991). Detail.*

▼

103

The Chamberlain Memorial Fountain
(John H. Chamberlain, no relation, 1880) stands in the centre of the square named after Joseph Chamberlain. Behind the memorial is the Museum and Art Gallery, which was designed by Yeoville Thomason and was opened by HRH the Prince of Wales on 28 November 1885.
◄

Thomas Attwood
(Sioban Coppinger, 1992). A reclining statue in Chamberlain Square close to the Town Hall. An earlier statue (John Thomas, 1859) is to be found in Sparkbrook.
▼

Chamberlain Square

There are several works of public art from Victorian times in Chamberlain Square. The Chamberlain Memorial Fountain was constructed from Portland stone and erected in 1880, shortly after Chamberlain left local Government to take up his seat in Parliament. There are also statues to James Watt and Joseph Priestley.

In 1993 a new sculpture of Thomas Attwood was sited in Chamberlain Square. The figure is cast in bronze and seen reclining on the steps of the square alongside a soap-box and sheets from one of the great politician's speeches. Born in Halesowen in 1783, Attwood was a Birmingham banker and MP. He founded the Birmingham Political Union which pressed for currency and parliamentary reform. He was a prime mover for the Reform Bill of 1832, which allowed Birmingham to elect two MPs, but he withdrew from public life after the Chartist Riots. By the time of his death he had fallen from favour and was largely forgotten. In more recent times his considerable influence on economic thinking and democratic reform has once again been recognized. An

THOMAS ATTWOOD
FOUNDER OF
THE BIRMINGHAM
POLITICAL

Compassion
(*Uli Nimptch, 1963*)
is to be found outside
the management
offices of Selly Oak
Hospital.

Heartlands Gateways.
The project to renew a 2350-
acre area to the north-east side
of the city includes a number
of new items of public art.

Face to Face
(*Ray Smith, 1993*)
Waterlinks Boulevard,
Aston
▶

Sleeping Iron Giant
(*Ondre Nowakowski, 1992*)
Garrison Lane,
Bordesley Green
▼

earlier statue of Thomas Attwood was moved from the city centre to Sparkbrook near the site of his house.

Out of Town

There are many further works of art all around Birmingham and new pieces seem to appear at regular intervals.

In particular in Heartlands, on the east side of the City, there is a series of new public art commissions at gateways to this development area.

▲
Entrance to
Bordesley Village.

◄

White Curl
(Suzi Gregory, 1993)
outside Waterlinks
House, Aston

Birmingham has recently taken significant steps to introduce new art for the public in the city, in a growing awareness that a pleasing city environment is very important in attracting both visitors and commerce. It is refreshing to see that this activity has been accomplished with both public and private funding. There are signs that all this effort is leading to an increasing appreciation of art by both the citizens of Birmingham and certainly by the increasing number of visitors to the city.

►
Firework Fantasia.
The City of Birmingham
Symphony Orchestra and
fireworks watched by a crowd
of 80,000 in Cannon Hill
Park in June 1992.

Chapter Eight

Sounds Like Birmingham

With the opening, in 1991, of Symphony Hall as part of the International Convention Centre, a long-standing Birmingham dream came true. Symphony Hall has awakened a wider Birmingham audience to music, raised the city's international status and is the crowning point of a musical tradition which goes back to the 1830s when Birmingham Town Hall was built specifically for musical events.

Birmingham was the UK City of Music in 1992 and during that year you could not turn a street corner without coming across a musical performance of some description. Today Birmingham continues to demonstrate the prestige and liveliness that high-quality musicians and venues can bring to a City.

Music for Hospitals

The Birmingham Triennial Music Festivals of the eighteenth century were an important society event. The first festival was held in 1768 and the triennial festivals began in 1784. Funds from the early concerts were used to help establish the General Hospital, the original purpose for which the festival was conceived. In a history of the festivals Bunce stated that they had 'done so much to make the name of Birmingham famous throughout Europe, as the cultivator and promoter of the

Carols for All in Birmingham Town Hall with the City of Birmingham Choir and The Heart of England Brass Ensemble, Conductor Christopher Robinson.

▼

musical art in its highest developments'. The early music festivals were generally held at St Philip's Church, now Birmingham's Anglican cathedral, and a theatre in New Street.

By the end of the eighteenth century the Birmingham Triennial Music Festival was established in the national social calendar. Indeed, pick-pockets were reported to travel from London especially for the event. They took advantage of the local ill-feeling against the new fashion for wearing shoelaces, which was dis-astrous for the Birmingham buckle trade. Pick-pockets hustled the wearers of shoe laces and in the chaos they, as Dent described, 'plied their calling vigorously, and managed to reap a good harvest'.

The attendance of the aristocracy at the festivals, meant that by the end of the eighteenth century nearly £6,000 had been raised towards the work of the General Hospital.

In 1834 the Festival was held in the new Town Hall for the first time. The building was not complete but was far enough advanced for the performances which, as always, included *Messiah.* Over the last 160 years, a number of historic musical events have occurred in the Town Hall. Two notable premières were Mendelssohn's *Elijah* in 1846 and Elgar's *The Dream of Gerontius* in 1900. The interior of the Hall was upgraded in 1926, when an additional gallery was installed. In 1994 major work on the fabric of the Town Hall was undertaken. From 1920 to 1991, Birmingham Town Hall was the home of the City of Birmingham Symphony Orchestra before it transferred to Symphony Hall.

The Town Hall organ was built by William Hill of London. It has over 4,000 pipes, four sets of keys and nearly eighty stops, with the longest pipe being thirty-five feet. Not surprisingly, it can produce a very wide range of tone and power.

Birmingham Town Hall.
The classical design of
Hansom and Welch forms one
side of Victoria Square.
Originally built to house the
Birmingham Triennial Music
Festival it opened in 1834 but
was not completed until 1850.

113

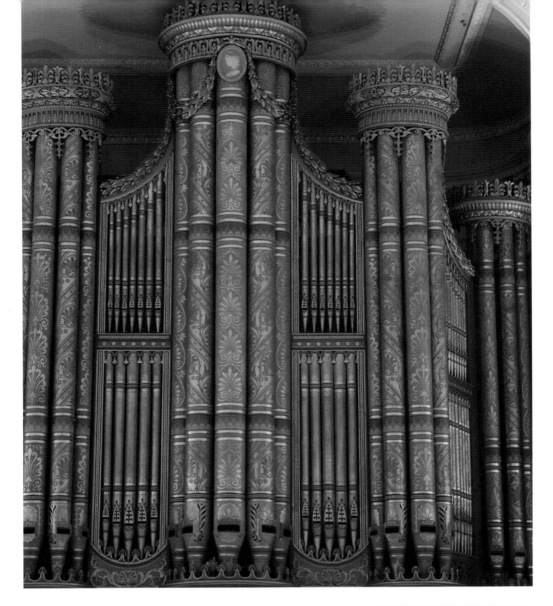

Mendelssohn played on the organ and the pipes still retain their original decoration.

City of Birmingham Symphony Orchestra

The City of Birmingham Orchestra was founded in 1920, by public figures such as Neville Chamberlain and the composer Granville Bantock; in 1948 'Symphony' was added to the name. The first symphony concert in the Town Hall was conducted by Sir Edward Elgar. During the 1920s and 1930s the orchestra became established as the major professional Midlands music group, under the direction of Adrian (later Sir Adrian) Boult and Leslie Heward. After the Second World War, George Weldon and Rudolf Schwarz were in command. The international prestige of the CBSO was much increased during the tenure of Hugo Rignold in the 1960s and Louis Frémaux in the 1970s with a number of overseas tours and recordings. In 1980 Simon Rattle became the Principal Conductor and Artistic Adviser to the CBSO and in 1990 its Music Director.

In 1925 the Principal Conductor, Adrian Boult, was promised a new concert hall; it took until 1991 for this promise to be fulfilled. However, many would say it was worth the wait. The orchestra plays around fifty-five concerts each year in Symphony Hall, many of them to capacity audiences.

The CBSO has its own Symphony Chorus and also plays regularly with the City of Birmingham Choir, both of which are made up of local people. Christopher Robinson has conducted the City of Birmingham Choir since 1964, and such continuity has enabled them to undertake some major choral works in recent times.

Symphony Hall

The opening of Symphony Hall in April 1991 marked a great achievement for Birmingham. Soon after opening, the hall was being compared to the very best in the world with some artists suggesting that it has the finest acoustics of them all; for the

▶

Symphony Hall
from the centre of the
platform.

◀

The City of Birmingham Symphony Orchestra with the CBSO Chorus, the City of Birmingham Choir, children from the School of St Mary and St Anne, Abbots Bromley and Shrewsbury Prep Schools, together with soloists, performing Mahler's Symphony No. 8 (Symphony of a Thousand). Mark Elder was the conductor for this spectacular performance on 5 February 1994.

117

listener it certainly has tremendous atmosphere. Symphony Hall has enabled Birmingham to host international orchestras and musicians and establish international musical associations which would have been impossible without such a venue. It has also played a key role in encouraging young musicians and local groups in the Midlands.

The acoustics of Symphony Hall were designed by the American, Russell Johnson of Artec Consultants. The shape of a concert hall is very

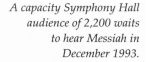

A capacity Symphony Hall audience of 2,200 waits to hear Messiah in December 1993.

Sir Simon Rattle joined the CBSO in 1980. In September 1998 he is succeeded by the Finnish conductor Sakari Oramo who becomes the tenth conductor to take charge of the CBSO.

important and a rectangular 'shoe-box' was chosen in line with classic halls such as the Musikverein in Vienna, the Concertgebouw in Amsterdam and Symphony Hall in Boston. The Birmingham Symphony Hall is constructed of heavy reinforced concrete, with dense surfaces of plaster and stone, which mimic the metre-thick walls of these nineteenth-century halls.

Symphony Hall always aimed to have fine acoustics, but these had to be adaptable to a huge range of events, from the largest orchestra playing the loudest work, to a small ensemble, and from popular music and speech, to conference lectures. A wider range of acoustical character is required for such a variety of events than would normally be found in one room. What makes Symphony Hall so exciting are the design features that enable the acoustics to be altered to give different effects for very different types of performance. Instant changes of this kind are achieved by control of three features: the reverberation chamber, the acoustic curtains and an acoustic canopy. These act to control the type and extent of the 'lateral' sound reflected off surfaces in the hall, rather than the sound coming direct from the source.

The reverberation chamber is a large space behind the platform rising the full height of the hall, where it joins additional chambers running along the sides of the hall. By opening and closing doors in the side chambers, significant changes in the 'liveness' of the sound can be achieved. For example music by Haydn or Mozart for smaller ensembles would have the chamber doors closed, while for a major orchestral work, such as Mahler, they would be open.

Acoustic curtains, or sliding screens of sound-absorbent material, are designed to control the audible 'tail'. They are used to deaden the hall acoustics for speech or when amplified sound systems are used.

In 1993 the Birmingham Early Music Festival staged events at a number of interesting places. Seen here are the Scottish Early Music Consort performing Monteverdi: Scenes of Love and War (The Battle of Tancredi and Clorinda) in the Victorian banking hall of the former Birmingham Town Bank. This was recently renovated and now forms part of the offices of Wragge and Co. in Colmore Row.

▼

The third and most visually dramatic component, is the acoustic canopy, suspended above the platform and front stalls. This changes the room acoustics and visual scale of the hall. It can be set as high as twenty-four metres above the stage, but for small-scale, intimate music the canopy can be set lower.

Widening Musical Appreciation

The Birmingham Early Music Festival and the Birmingham Contemporary Music Group are just two of many examples of musical enterprises that are benefiting from Birmingham's increased musical vitality and a growing interest in live music. The Birmingham Contemporary Music Group was formed in 1987 by players from the CBSO, with Simon Rattle as Artistic Adviser. They quickly became known as a leading contemporary music ensemble and have as a central aim the commissioning and performance of new music.

Ronnie Scott's Jazz Club on Broad Street, just a short distance from the ICC, is an important venue for the annual Birmingham Jazz Festival. There are also a number of other pubs and clubs in the city where live music is played all year round. Birmingham Jazz is an organisation which promotes contemporary jazz in the city. In conjunction with the Birmingham Contemporary Music Group they produce 'The Series' which is a season of concerts designed to promote the best of contemporary jazz and classical music. In 1993 The Series won the Prudential Award for Music with the judges citing '..its refreshing disregard for the usual boundaries of music..'.

The 150th Anniversary of the performance of Elijah *in Birmingham by the Birmingham Festival Choral Sociey in St Philip's Cathedral.*

Sounds Like Birmingham. *Music is fun and in Birmingham there can be a lot of it about!*

Top row (left to right)

- *Ronnie Scott in person.*
- *Nachda Sansaar perform at Birmingham Town Hall.*
- *Last Practice; CBSO harpist Robert Johnston tunes up prior to the Firework Fantasia.*

Middle row (left to right)

- *Spirit of the Earth, Chamberlain Square.*
- *The Eureka Jazz Band, Sparkhill Park Fun Day.*

Bottom Row (left to right)

- *The Birmingham Bach Choir and Orchestra with Conductor Paul Spicer in the Adrian Boult Hall.*
- *The Maestros Steel Band at Birmingham Town Hall.*
- *Music in the City Plaza.*
- *A busking competition gives a curious air of respectability to this craft.*

Sounds Like Birmingham

In 1992 Birmingham was chosen by the Arts Council as host for the first Arts 2000 project. The aim was to fill the year with high-quality music of every form, including formal occasions and open-air events - from busking on the street to the CBSO Firework Fantasia at Cannon Hill Park, attended by a crowd of 80,000 people.

Birmingham has realised just how powerful music can be in enhancing the city's image. There were those who doubted that Symphony Hall could succeed, with such a substantial increase in capacity compared with the Town Hall, but, after breaking box office records and spearheading renewed interest in all forms of music, Symphony Hall has clearly been a remarkable achievement for the City of Birmingham.

▲

The Tim Amann Quartet playing on a Sunday lunchtime at the Strathallan Hotel, Hagley Road. This weekly session is staged jointly with the hotel, Birmingham Jazz and the Musicians' Union.

▶

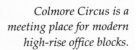

Colmore Circus is a meeting place for modern high-rise office blocks.

Chapter Nine

Twentieth-Century
Industry and Commerce

Towards the end of the nineteenth century the population of Birmingham was approaching 250,000 and the town expanding fast. The great industrial diversity of the city was still mainly based on traditional metal-working and engineering skills. Birmingham dominated the world market in areas such as pen-nib manufacture, brass products of all descriptions and a wide variety of other household goods. Industry still relied largely on small workshops and in 1870 there were thought to be less than twenty firms employing more than 500 people, with as many as 7,000 smaller workshops. This was soon to change as other countries started to compete in many of Birmingham's traditional markets.

With the coming of the twentieth century increasing mechanisation often required fewer skilled workers and payment changed from piece pay to pay by the hour. Trades unions were formed to negotiate terms and conditions and to demand safer workplaces. At the same time, smaller firms amalgamated to form larger concerns to gain a commercial advantage by economy of scale. New industries included bicycle production and their components and later motorcycles and then, of course, cars. By the 1880s, bicycle production was very important, with the brass and tube manufacturers of Birmingham taking up this product, and the Birmingham Small Arms company (BSA) producing bicycles as an alternative to armaments. There were also many manufacturers producing bicycle components - for example Joseph Lucas, a Birmingham lamp-maker with his 'King of the Road' lamp. By 1911, there were approaching 10,000 people in Birmingham employed in bicycle manufacturing.

Wartime Production

The First and Second World wars were periods of major industrial activity in the City. Before 1914 the BSA company was making 135 rifles a week but during the First World War this rose to 10,000.

Hot brass at Aerospace Forgings Oldbury.
Hot forging is a mixture of getting the conditions right together with skill and experience. This component is destined for the UK aircraft industry.

▲ ▶

The original Lucas works in Newtown is marked with a granite memorial. The King Street factory, seen behind, was demolished in 1994 as part of the City Challenge scheme to redevelop this part of the City.

▼

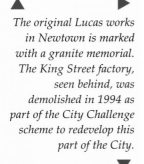

In the factories of Joseph Lucas the First World War was also a period of major expansion as they made magnetos, lamps, shell covers, self-starters, dynamos and other electrical goods. The Kynoch factory at Witton became a huge centre for manufacture of ammunition and this is now part of the IMI plc site. At the peak of the war 18,000 people, many of them women known locally as 'Kynoch's Angels', worked at the factory, producing over 30 million rounds of ammunition a week. Wartime also saw women entering the industrial workforce in a major way.

Between the First and Second World wars, Birmingham factories continued to develop conveyor-belt and assembly-line practices, with factories designed to produce very large quantities of goods as economically as possible. This inter-war period was one of high unemployment and recession but this changed in the mid-1930s with the build-up to the Second World War. As war became more likely new 'shadow' factories were built alongside the conventional factories, and four were built around Birmingham - two managed by the Rover company at Acocks Green and Solihull, a third alongside the Austin factory at Longbridge. The Nuffield shadow factory at Castle Bromwich produced over 11,000 Spitfires and 300 Lancasters during the war. Other firms converted their production to help the war effort. Firms such as Cadbury began to make aeroplane parts as did many much smaller concerns in the Jewellery Quarter.

As a very important industrial area, Birmingham was subjected to heavy aerial bombardment during the Second World War and only London and Liverpool suffered more attacks. On the night of 19 November 1940, in an air raid seemingly aimed at the BSA factory at Small Heath, 350 German bombers got through to Birmingham. That night nearly 400 people died in the city, over fifty of them at the BSA factory itself.

Motor-car City

Birmingham is still a centre for car assembly and component production and has a wealth of automobile engineering expertise. On several occasions, the city has introduced radical thinking into car design, which has been influential on a world scale.

At the end of the nineteenth century the manufac-ture of motor-cars was becoming important in Birmingham and the Austin factory at Longbridge is an excellent example of this development. Herbert Austin built his first car in 1895, while employed at the Wolseley Sheep Shearing Machine Company. Austin's first four-wheel car was the

Wolseley Voiturette and this single-cylinder, five-horsepower car won a public trial over 1,000 miles in 1900. In 1905, the Austin Motor Company was formed and Herbert Austin bought the site of a disused printing works at Longbridge, five miles from Birmingham City Centre and close to the Lickey Hills. The company's first car was produced in 1906 and by 1914, 2,000 workers were employed at the factory, producing 1500 cars per year.

In 1921, because of post-war financial difficulties, the Austin Motor Company went into receivership. A management committee of shareholders

On August Bank Holiday 1992 hundreds of Austin Seven cars returned to Longbridge for a tour of their birthplace.

▼

and the Midland Bank took over the running of the firm. Using his private resources, Austin secretly developed the Austin Seven in the converted billiard room at his home Lickey Grange with his assistant, the seventeen-year-old designer Stanley Edge, who had been trained at the Austin works. For eight months, the two men set about designing a low-cost mass-produced car to realise Austin's ambition to 'motorise the masses'. Production started in 1922 and the Austin Seven initially cost £225, though as production rose the price fell to £168. Between 1922 and the beginning of the Second World War approximately 300,000 Austin Sevens were produced and the Seven was also manufactured under licence in various parts of the world. Indeed the Austin Seven design was the first car that BMW produced. Its success lay in providing reasonable reliability and comfort. The accepted body shape was inexpensively made from steel pressings resulting in a low-cost car which sold well.

In the 1950s a second great design change emanated from Longbridge. Alex Issigonis led a team looking at the small car market with a brief to produce a small economical car, capable of carrying four people in reasonable comfort. The result was the Mini, launched in 1960, whose radical design featured a space-saving transverse-

The Range Rover has been a continuing success story despite a number of changes of ownership of the Solihull based factory.

A short wheelbase Land Rover crosses the River Cole at Hall Green.

mounted engine, and front-wheel drive. Transverse engines and front-wheel drive are now standard elements of modern car design, but at that time they were revolutionary.

Since the development of the Mini, the Birmingham automotive industry has undergone many changes, and, like the motorcycle industry, it has been dogged by insufficient long-term investment in modern design and production processes, restrictive working practices and overmanning. The Austin name was finally lost in 1989, when British Aerospace took over the company with the formation of their Rover car division and this was sold to the German company BMW on 31 January 1994.

The car industry in Birmingham now concentrates on the high-quality end of the market. The Solihull-based Land Rover factory produces four-wheel-drive cars such as the Range Rover, Discovery and Defender, which are all extremely successful. The original Land Rover was launched at the Amsterdam Motor Show in 1948; it cost £450 and to start with doors came as an optional extra. Since then over 1.5 million Land Rovers have been sold.

LDV Assembly Line, Washwood Heath.
LDV was formed as a management buy-out after the financial collapse of the Dutch Daf company in 1993. LDV has retained important skills and the staff show a dedication and sense of purpose that makes one optimistic for the future of manufacturing enterprise in Birmingham.

Birmingham Banks and Commerce

Since the eighteenth century, industrial activity in Birmingham has required substantial financing which led to the establishment of a number of banks in the city, the best known today being Lloyds and the Midland Bank. Before the advent of commercial banks, it was the practice for merchants to lend money to manufacturers to buy raw materials and pay their workers' wages. Often industrial entrepreneurs themselves sought wealthy business partners and in some cases, such as that of Matthew Boulton, they were lucky enough to have some finance of their own.

New industries were sometimes started when profits from another area of work were re-invested in new projects. Josiah Mason used his fortune made from split-ring production to start large-scale pen manufacturing, and the printing business of John Baskerville was sustained on the profits from his japanning business.

'Farm', Sparkbrook, dating from the mid-18th century, was the home of the original Lloyd's Bank family. The house survived the Priestley Riots of 1791 and is an excellent example of Birmingham architecture of the period.

▶

Prestige office buildings on Colmore Row as seen from the cupola of St Philip's Cathedral with the Telecom Tower behind.

▼

▲

*The Bennett's Hill branch of
the Midland Bank by the
architect Thomas Rickman
dates from 1830. It started out
as the Birmingham Banking
Company, that company's
initials still being seen over
the entrance, becoming part of
the Midland Bank in 1914.*

The first Sampson Lloyd came to Birmingham from mid-Wales in 1698 and developed a successful iron business. His family founded Taylor and Lloyds bank with John Taylor, who had made his fortune as a maker of gilt-metal buttons and enamelled snuff boxes. Their first bank was in Dale End with the head office of what later became Lloyd's Bank in Colmore Row.

William Hutton spoke of the start of this Birmingham bank as follows: '... about every tenth trader was a banker or a retailer of cash. ... a regular bank was established in 1765 by Taylor and Lloyd, two opulent tradesmen whose credit being equal to the bank of England, quickly collected the shining rays of sterling into focus.'

The bank moved its headquarters to London in 1884 and the oldest branch still open in the centre of Birmingham is in Temple Row, close to St Philip's Cathedral. The family home was Lloyd's Farm in Sparkbrook. This building survived the

Priestley Riots of 1791 and, much more recently, several years of inner-city decay. It was renovated in the 1980s and is now the headquarters for a Birmingham housing association.

The Midland Bank, originally the Birmingham and Midland Bank, was founded in 1836 and had its headquarters in Birmingham until 1891. The original 1869 head office has recently been renovated and is now a bookshop, on the corner of New Street and Stephenson Place.

City 2000, the financial services promotional organisation, works alongside the Birmingham Marketing Partnership and Birmingham Chamber of Commerce and Industry to promote the city. Birmingham is a regional centre, and this is reflected in the major corporate names in banking, insurance, accountancy and other professions who have offices in the city.

Birmingham International Airport is at Bickenhill, just a 10-minute rail ride from the centre of the city. The NEC opened in 1976 and has been expanding ever since. Besides being a major centre for exhibitions and conferences the NEC also stages large pop concerts.

Today the infrastructure of the commercial district of Birmingham is undergoing regeneration. Modern office premises are being produced, both by the refurbishment of existing buildings and the construction of brand new buildings. In the city centre, Colmore Row is a fine example of what can be done by making use of existing Victorian build-

ings and upgrading them for modern office use. The Colmore Row offices of Wragge & Co. are an excellent example of prestige office space, developed from such original Victorian architecture. At the Snow Hill end of Colmore Row is a group of modern office buildings, with Colmore Gate and The Wesleyan certainly being eye-catching. Close by, the former Lewis's department store has been converted to a further large office development called Temple Court.

Exhibitions and Conventions

In the 1970s it was decided to build the National Exhibition Centre, (NEC), to the east of the city, at Bickenhill, next to Birmingham airport. The first phase was opened in 1976 and the centre has been a continuing success, with further development of the site ensuring that the NEC is a leading venue for exhibitions of all descriptions, including the British Motor Show. The NEC Arena has also been very successful at staging large musical events.

An exhibition of hospital laboratory equipment at the Association of Clinical Biochemists' Annual meeting in April 1993.

Building on the experience of the NEC and faced with a declining industrial base, Birmingham decided to extend the NEC concept with a convention centre of international standing, right in the heart of Birmingham. The site chosen was that of the old Bingley Hall, on Broad Street, which had

Cadbury World gives an excellent introduction to chocolate-making at the Bournville factory. Seen here is a replica of the Bull Street shop opened by John Cadbury in 1824. The tour of Cadbury World includes demonstrations of hand-made chocolate production.

been erected in 1850, and was an innovative exhibition hall in its time, capable of holding 20,000 people. Construction of the International Convention Centre (ICC) began in 1986, opening for business on 2 April 1991. The ICC is used for meetings and exhibitions of all descriptions, from a small group of half a dozen, to a large congress with associated exhibitions and many thousands of delegates. Marketing a conference venue is a long-term business; international congresses are often booked many years in advance. Birmingham entered this market during the continuing recession of the late 1980s and so far has done well to bring a significant number of world congresses to the city.

Financing Change

In the nineteenth century, Joseph Chamberlain financed his municipal revolution with, amongst other things, profits from the Corporation gas works. Today, such finance is not available and the major investment for new civic projects has come from the City Council, who have been successful in obtaining grants from the European Community to help with much of the new development. In the late 1980s, EC grants totalling £143 million were used to help with projects like the ICC, an exten-sion to the NEC, Aston Science Park and city-centre pedestrianisation. A second phase of £32 million is being used for initiatives such as the regeneration of inner city areas, transport schemes including the upgrading of Birmingham Airport, and projects to help tourism and the city environment.

Investment by private enterprise is an important feature of new projects. The Heartlands Development Corporation is a fine example of public and private enterprise working together. Heartlands is the name for a 2,350 acre area to the north-east of the city centre, which is undergoing extensive and co-ordinated redevelopment, with a mixture of new industrial, office and residential projects as well as the upgrading of existing housing.

Part of the Heartlands project, Bordesley Village, is a development of private and public housing which makes living in the inner city an attractive proposition. This new housing is complemented by a pleasing park environment and the design aims to minimise the old problems associated with

Old Turn Junction is lit up by the 1996 New Year's Eve fireworks. ◀

Bordesley Village.
New housing in the inner
city is designed to minimise
problems previously
associated with inner-city
life. This is part of the
Heartlands development
which is an integrated
programme to regenerate
a large inner city area.

inner-city life. Waterlinks is a canalside business village which demonstrates how the Birmingham canals are being incorporated into interesting new commercial premises.

The economy of Birmingham is still changing, from a predominantly industrialised manufacturing centre, to a much more mixed economy. Although innovations such as the NEC and ICC may be considered part of the service sector, they are also helpful in giving prestige and back-up to the city, which should encourage inward investment in the manufacturing sectors and thus further strengthen the local economy. Birmingham's engineering expertise is a very valuable resource. Despite the difficult economic climate of the 1980s and the loss of many manufacturing jobs, engineering expertise must surely form an important part of the continuing renewal of Birmingham into the twenty-first century.

▶

Tours of the City operate
in the summer months.

The Edwardian Tea Rooms,
Birmingham Museum and
Art Gallery.

Jalebi manufacture at the
Vaisakhi Sikh Festival in
Handsworth Park.

The 1994 Birmingham to
Oxford bike ride leaves
the NEC.

Chapter Ten
Life in the City

Birmingham is a green city, full of tree-lined roads, parks and other open spaces and there is a great deal to see and do. This book is no more than a personal glimpse of Birmingham, its history, people and ways of life, through images of the present-day city.

University Life in Birmingham

There are three Universities in the city: Birmingham University, at Edgbaston, Aston University with its campus close to the city centre and the University of Central England (UCE) based at Perry Barr but with departments in various parts of the city. The total student population reading for degrees at the three universities is now over 30,000 and is expected to rise over the next few years.

Fun on the Streets

The EC summit which took place on 16 October 1992 was an excellent example of the Birmingham

Cannon Hill Park is one of many open spaces in the City.

▼

'Old Joe' is named after Joseph Chamberlain and is a dominant feature in the centre of Birmingham University.

145

◄

Expect the unexpected in Birmingham. Here is street theatre on the EC summit day, 16 October 1992.

approach to life. While the European Heads of State met inside the International Convention Centre, the media 'pack' were entertained outside by jugglers on stilts, clowns, street theatre groups everywhere, and activists of all descriptions. This was a day to be remembered on the streets of Birmingham.

There are many organised public events in the parks of Birmingham each year, probably the biggest and most colourful is Handsworth Carnival, held in early September. Carnival first came to Birmingham in 1983. For an entire weekend Handsworth Park reverberates to the sound of music and the carnival parade itself is mainly on foot in true Caribbean style and with a great feeling of fun.

Birmingham for a New Beginning

Immigration has always been important to Birmingham's growth and development. Even some of the Welsh stonemasons who brought the Anglesey marble to build the Town Hall in the 1830s decided to settle in the town. Higher wages drew workers into Birmingham from the surrounding agricultural areas and between 1801 and 1831 the population of Birmingham nearly doubled.

▶

The 1993 Handsworth Carnival. *Handsworth Park is turned over to a giant party and the smells of traditional Caribbean cooking.*

On the chalkboard menu in the lower left image:

JAMAICA
MENUE
JERK CHICKEN
WITH RICE AND PEA
JERK CHICKEN WITH
BREAD
JERK CHICKEN WITH
SALAD AND COLDSLAW
CHICKEN CHOW MEIN
CURRY CHICKEN WITH
RICE
SPAIR RIBS
SWEETCORN
ACKIE AND SALTFISH
FRIED DUMPLING
FESTIVAL DUMPLING
FRIED PLANTING
FRITTERS

The most recent figures, from the 1991 census for the make-up of the Birmingham population, defined by ethnic groups are:

Ethnic Origin	No. of People	%
White	754,274	78.5
Pakistani	66,085	6.9
Indian	51,075	5.3
Black Caribbean	44,770	4.7
Bangladeshi	12,739	1.3
Black Other	11,606	1.2
Other (non-white)	20,492	2.1
Total	**961,041**	**100%**

During the twentieth century Birmingham has been a natural centre to come and settle in, offering comparatively good employment opportunities in both the manufacturing and service sectors, as well as opportunities to start new businesses. It has the largest ethnic minority population in a British city with just over 20 per cent of the city's nearly one million inhabitants being of non-white origin, compared with a national average of about 5 per cent. Such a wide range of cultural backgrounds adds new dimensions to the city's life. Indeed, Birmingham has worked hard to ensure that people understand and appreciate the different cultures that surround them.

Birmingham Hippodrome, the home of the Birmingham Royal Ballet, is in the middle of the Chinese Quarter with many popular Chinese restaurants all around.

Interestingly, the Birmingham Chinese population is just 0.3 per cent of the total but has a high profile. A Chinese Quarter close to the Hippodrome contains many Chinese businesses including restaurants and suppliers to the Chinese catering trade. Indeed, the cultural diversity of Birmingham has led to a wide range of food to enjoy when eating out. Of all the tastes to be found, the most celebrated is surely the Balti Curry.

Going for a Balti

If you pick up a British Sunday newspaper or turn on Breakfast TV in the 1990s, you are as likely to see a review of the Birmingham Balti phenomenon as you are of the redevelopment of Birmingham city centre or the new public art. Balti Curry has reached cult status and has spread from Birmingham to other Midlands towns, London and beyond.

A Balti is literally a metal dish with two handles, similar to a small wok, in which a Balti Curry should be cooked and served. In Birmingham this type of cooking originates mainly from the Sparkbrook and Sparkhill areas of the inner city but is now found all over Birmingham. Many of the original Balti Houses were established along Stoney Lane, Ladypool Road and the Stratford Road just to the south of the city centre. Originals such as Saleems and Adils have been joined by an increasing number of newer restaurants. As branches of banks close down on the Stratford Road they are converted to Balti restaurants almost overnight. A traditional Balti House or Sweet Centre has Asian sweets in the window and a simple restaurant area behind. A Balti is usually eaten with nan bread, used to scoop up the curry, and almost never with rice.

Balti House Cuisine.
From raw ingredients to finished product.
▶

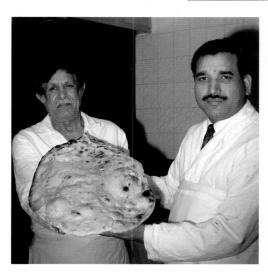

Balti cooking is thought to have its origins in the Indian North-West Frontier and to have spread from there to the Kashmir and Punjab regions. Spices such as coriander, cardamom, ginger, fennel and cumin are all basic ingredients. Original Balti cooking produced a dry dish, but the Birmingham version has been Westernised by the addition of a sauce.

The success of the Balti is surely due to a combination of several factors. Balti cooking can be very pleasant on the taste-buds, the atmosphere of a Balti House is very relaxing and eating out Balti-style can be extremely cheap. In the 1990s new up-market restaurants in the city centre are using the Balti name and they should create even more interest in the original downtown Balti establishments.

First Class Football and Cricket

There are three major football teams in the City. Aston Villa have their ground at Villa Park, built on part of the original Aston Hall grounds. Birmingham City is based at St Andrew's, set on high ground to the east of the City and West Bromwich Albion's ground is based at the

Birmingham City, known as 'The Blues' play at St Andrew's. ▼

Warwickshire cricket ground with Cannon Hill Park in the foreground

Hawthorns just across the city border in Sandwell. Changes in ground safety regulations have demanded substantial investment in all three grounds which now have fine all-seater stadiums.

Edgbaston is the home of Warwickshire Cricket Club and is also a regular venue for test matches. The ground was established on the banks of the River Rea, where cricket has been played since the first major match against the MCC in June 1886.

International Sporting Events

The National Indoor Arena and National Exhibition Centre provide venues for important sporting events. Since its opening the NIA has seen major World and European championships in such diverse events as netball, men's powerlifting, climbing and badminton. It has certainly proved a very adaptable venue and the country's only 200 metre six-lane demountable track has already had many world records broken on it.

Besides sporting events the NIA has also hosted large-scale entertainment events from grand operatic productions to ice spectaculars and the Sir Cliff Richard musical *Heathcliffe*. It is also the

The National Indoor Arena is home to the popular Gladiators television programme.
◀

home of the popular *Gladiators* programme which is filmed there each summer, attracting up to 13 million viewers per show. The NIA has also become the home of the Birmingham Bullets basketball team.

Sailboarding at Bartley Green Reservoir
▶

Sport for All

For those who wish to take part in sport rather than just watch, Birmingham has excellent facilities. There are numerous well-used sports centres throughout the city and a number of municipal golf courses that don't require membership and sailing clubs on a number of reservoirs. Sutton Park is an amazing resource where all these activities are available and one can even join the model aeroplane club or spend the day walking this great expanse of open space.

Sport for all:
Moseley Rugby Club play at 'The Reddings' in Moseley.

The Birmingham Bullets basketball team play at the National Indoor Arena.

Solihull Blaze ice hockey team have a dedicated following.
▼

Positively Birmingham

Birmingham's people have always thrived on change. In the twelfth century they created a bustling market town. The eighteenth century saw a huge surge in industrial activity. In the nineteenth century the city led the way in the drive for decent living conditions. Twentieth century Birmingham has been an industrial world leader.

Today, Birmingham's people face another period of change; large in scale but harder to define. Fine new buildings and contemporary art go hand in hand with the re-discovery and regeneration of architectural heritage and industrial tradition, to create an exciting, prosperous and thriving city.

Above all else Birmingham has succeeded because of the skills, enterprise and positive attitude of the people who have chosen to live in the city. In this positive attitude lies the key to the future.

▲

The Birmingham Wheels Project in Bordesley is in the Heartlands Development area.

Birmingham Botanical Gardens are fun for children too.

◄

The International Convention Centre Mall now forms a pedestrian link between the city centre squares and Brindleyplace.

►

Chapter Eleven

Towards the Millennium

As the end of the twentieth century approaches Birmingham would be justified in feeling satisfied at some of its major new developments and might sit back to enjoy the global party. Instead Birmingham is striving forward and at an increasing pace with exciting building projects all over the city.

, The Brindleyplace development opposite the International Convention Centre is now a major urban quarter with business accommodation, housing, leisure, entertainment and retail facilities, and includes another square complete with public art. *Aqueduct*, (Miles Davies, 1995), is twenty feet high, weighs eleven tons and is made of phosphor

Curzon Street railway station was the terminus of the London to Birmingham railway (Philip Hardwick, 1838). This historic architectural memorial to railway pioneers is now to be included in the Millennium Point Project.

▲

The National Sealife Centre opened at Brindleyplace in the summer of 1996 and includes a 360° walk-through tunnel from which the sharks can be viewed.

bronze. The Ikon Gallery moves to the old Oozells Street School (Martin & Chamberlain, 1877) in 1997 with the help of the Arts Lottery Fund and the Crescent Theatre will soon be moving to a new building on a corner of the canal. The Brindleyplace development and the International Convention Centre have encouraged considerable inward investment around Broad Street and it is difficult to remember what a run-down part of the city this used to be.

Digbeth Goes High-Tech

In October 1996 the announcement of £50 million of National Lottery money from the Millennium Commission secured a public/private sector initia-

The Water's Edge at Brindleyplace is a popular place to eat.

▶

▲

From the air the area of Digbeth and Deritend show their relationship to the rest of the city centre.

tive to kick-start the redevelopment of Digbeth. Millennium Point is a science-based multi-faceted project on a twenty-five acre site around Curzon Street station. As well as the £50 million from the Millennium Commission this £110 million development has funding coming from the European Commission (£22 million), from Birmingham City Council, the private sector and the regeneration agency English Partnerships (£12.5 million).

The Millennium Point concept contains a number of elements. The Discovery Centre will celebrate the scientific and technological achievements of Birmingham and the West Midlands and look at future developments. It will use new-style interactive technology and virtual reality simulations and house exhibits currently in the Museum of Science and Industry in Newhall Street. The overall aim is to make science and technology fun to experience. Anyone who has seen how much young people enjoy the Light on Science gallery at Newhall Street will appreciate the enormous potential for this approach.

The University of the First Age will provide educational opportunities for upwards of 90,000 young people, becoming the centre of a regional electronic network linking schools, colleges, libraries, homes and workplaces - all Birmingham schools will be electronically linked to the University.

Newer exhibits at the Museum of Science and Industry are an example of the hands-on approach which will be taken at the new Discovery Centre.

▼

The Technology Innovation Centre is an initiative led by the University of Central England (UCE) in collaboration with the city's other two universities. It will house the UCE Engineering and Computer Faculty and aims to be a centre of excellence for technology and innovation with emphasis on access and participation by young people, the general public and industry. The aim is that teaching facilities will be used by a diverse range of educational and commercial partners. The Hub will be a social centre which will include shops, cafes, an electronic library and conference rooms. Millennium Point is expected to create 1600 jobs directly and to attract half a million visitors a year. It will act as a focus for further private-sector redevelopment in the area, just as the International Convention Centre has done for Broad Street.

Bull Ring Redevelopment

The Bull Ring is to many people the heart of Birmingham and redevelopment of this run-down part of the city has been at the planning stage for many years. In 1990 proposals included demolishing the Rotunda to make way for a major 30-storey

The Rotunda was designed by James Roberts, and is an icon to the 1960s wealth of Birmingham. It is now to be integrated into redevelopment of the Bull Ring area of the city.

▶

161

office building, but economic recession put these always controversial plans on hold and gave time to work out new proposals which local people feel happier with.

Re-development of the Bull Ring includes the demolition of the 1960s centre and building a major new shopping complex. A new public square will surround St Martin's Church and the Rotunda will stay.

Custard Factory

The home of Bird's Custard on the banks of the River Rea in Digbeth High Street is today being developed as the Custard Factory Arts and Media Complex. The owner, Bennie Gray, is an innovative developer whose other major project in Birmingham has been the 'Big Peg' in the Jewellery Quarter. The first phase of the Custard Factory project was the conversion of Scott House into studios and offices, and this now houses over 130 companies with employment for around 350 people. The next phase proposes a giant modernistic building - the Greenhouse - and in total eight areas of development, including the creation of 'Custard Court' and the proposed redevelopment of the city's oldest library on Gibb Street.

The Custard Factory, originally the home of Bird's Custard, is now the successful home to new companies specialising in media and the arts.
▶

Children from the Nelson Mandela School in Sparkhill filming for a children's TV programme at the Custard Factory.
▼

Exciting Car Industry Developments

The investment in the Birmingham automotive industry continues at an increasing rate. Alongside the M6 in Heartlands a new Jaguar plant is being built which will start production of the new Mini-Jaguar, code-named the X200, in 1998. The new Jaguar could triple annual production and will itself create a thousand new jobs and many more with local component suppliers. Coventry-based Jaguar has a long association with Birmingham

The XK8 is a worthy successor to the E-Type Jaguar and has a new V8 engine.

Three 4 x 4 vehicles produced by Rover at their Solihull plant (left to right: Range Rover, Discovery and original Land Rover Defender) are to be joined in 1998 by a compact sports version.

▲

*The LDV concept Minibus,
shown here at the 1996
Motorshow at the NEC.*

with all their car bodies being produced at its Castle Bromwich plant. The company, now owned by Ford, has had considerable success with its new saloon. The XK8 sports went onto the market in 1996 and to many this is seen as the successor to the revered E-Type Jaguar.

Investment in the Rover Group factories continues apace under the ownership of BMW. The Land Rover factory in Solihull will produce a new compact 4 x 4 sports utility vehicle in 1998. Substantial investment in both plant and jobs is taking place, with continuing expansion of the workforce, and the factory has the largest paint shop in Europe. A new £400 million engine plant to produce engines to power both Rover and BMW cars is being constructed on the site of the former Hams Hall power station in Warwickshire.

The Longbridge built Mini has been voted 'car of the century' and approaches its fortieth birthday with a replacement under development. The long-standing success of the Mini is remarkable

*John Cooper helped launch the
1997 version of the Mini
Cooper at the Motorshow.*

▶

◄

The Longbridge-built MGF is a two seater, mid-engined sports car. It came onto the market in 1995 and has been a considerable success.

and the current Mini Cooper is increasingly being marketed as a trendy design statement; the fortieth birthday special edition will certainly be much sought after. The new Mini is being designed at Rover's Gaydon headquarters at a cost of £400 million and sales of up to 200,000 a year are projected for the car world-wide.

The MGF is a mid-engined, two seater sports car built at Longbridge. It was launched in 1995 and the waiting list for the car ensures full production far into the future. This is a car worthy of the Morris Garages name and carries on the tradition of providing exciting yet affordable motoring.

Birmingham is currently of growing importance as a centre for the European automotive industry offering a range of assembly plants and a strong component industry. Innovation has historically been a feature of Birmingham's approach to car manufacture and this should be nurtured further by newer overseas owners.

Transportation Policies for Birmingham

With the predicted growth of traffic on West Midlands roads major investment in the public transport infrastructure will be needed to avoid grid-lock. Traffic congestion is estimated to cost West Midlands businesses £1.5 billion per annum at present and the region has the highest

►

The A38M with the City Centre ahead.

New Street Station is in the centre of the city.

rush-hour traffic outside London This brings not only travel delays but also serious health, safety and environmental problems. A clear strategy to meet the needs of both public and private transport is urgently needed in Birmingham.

At last the light railway network, proposed for many years, has started to become a reality. Midland Metro Line 1 is supported by a Government grant (£40 million) and approved loan (£40 million) and a grant from the European Commission (£31 million) through its Regional Development Fund. Further local investment and money from private backers gives a total investment of £145 million. Midland Metro Line 1 between Birmingham Snow Hill and Wolverhampton's Market Street opens at the end of 1998. The line makes use of the old Great Western Railway route for 18 km of its 20 km length. The light rail system can transfer from dedicated rail routes to normal roads and Line 1 will join the highway at Monmore Green for the final 2 km to Wolverhampton. Parliamentary approval for two further routes has already been given, but the finance for these still has to be found.

Birmingham has introduced cycle routes into the City. These have been successful when they are separated from the road system, for example canal towpaths and the route along the River Rea. However, anyone who has tried to cycle into the central area of Birmingham appreciates how difficult cycling in a city can be. Increasingly the

There has been more emphasis on cycling in the city recently.

cycling lobby is losing patience with the poor cycling environment and on occasions activists exercise their right to cycle round the inner ring road which brings rush-hour traffic to a halt.

Travelling into Birmingham by coach has for many years been an experience one would rather forget. Digbeth Coach Station is a disaster for everyone, including those who come to pick people up and return to their cars to find them wheel-clamped by modern-day highwaymen. A new coach station is now a high priority for city planners.

New Street is now pedestrianised, with space for street evangelism and even the occasional human statue!

▼

City Centre Shopping Fights back

The centre of Birmingham, like many old-style city-centre shopping areas, has faced increasing competition from out-of-town shopping malls. However, the city is fighting back and city-centre pedestrianisation has been important in helping to make central Birmingham a more attractive place to shop, and a City Retail Group works to promote city-centre shopping. Birmingham city centre has also seen considerable private investment in upgrading older retail areas on Corporation Street and New Street and more upmarket shops are being attracted into the city. An excellent example is the creation of the Burlington Arcade from the old Burlington Passage with its suspended glass roof. This is part of an extensive improvement of the old Midland Hotel, which is now re-named the Burlington Hotel.

Changing Perceptions of Birmingham

Birmingham is quite distinct in character from London and comparisons to the capital are neither relevant nor helpful. It was unfortunate that in an earlier age Birmingham used the 'Second City' slogan to promote itself. In the 1990s the city has marketed itself in determined and novel ways with the Birmingham Marketing Partnership, Birmingham Chamber of Commerce & Industry and the financial services pressure group City 2000, along with others all working to promote the

The Birmingham Marketing Partnership offices (Goddard & Paget, 1904) on the edge of Victoria Square. The Birmingham 'wordmark' is displayed in the windows.

city. With the slogan 'Europe's Meeting Place' and using corporate marketing techniques, these organisations have succeeded in giving the city a high profile. Such efforts have to battle hard against the London-based national media and misconceptions of people who do not understand Birmingham.

When people experience Birmingham for themselves pre-conceived ideas change quickly. New attractions such as the National Sealife Centre, National Indoor Arena and International Convention Centre bring a very large number of visitors to the city and this can only speed this process. Gradually the world is discovering for itself what Birmingham's citizens have long taken for granted . . . this city is a good place to call home.

Bibliography

The following are some of the sources used for *Positively Birmingham*. They will be of interest if you would like to read in more depth or are researching aspects of Birmingham.

Briggs, Asa, *History of Birmingham* vol II, Oxford University Press, 1952

Church, Roy, *Herbert Austin: The British Motor Car Industry to 1941*, Europa Publications, London, 1979.

Dent, Robert, *Old and New Birmingham*, Houghton & Hammond, Birmingham, 1880.

Dent, Robert, *The Making of Birmingham*. J.L. Allday, Birmingham, 1894.

Fairclough, Oliver, *The Grand Old Mansion: The Holtes and Their Successors at Aston Hall 1618-1864*, Birmingham Museums and Art Gallery, 1984.

Foster, Richard, *Birmingham New Street; Background and Beginnings*, Chapter 2 'Birmingham's Canals', Wild Swan Publications, Didcot, 1990.

Gill, Conrad, *History of Birmingham* vol I, Oxford University Press, 1952.

Gledhill, Alison, *Birmingham's Jewellery Quarter*, K.A.F. Brewin Books, Studley, Warwickshire, 1988.

Haddleton, Marie, *The Jewellery Quarter: History and Guide*, YBA Publications, Birmingham, 1987.

Holyoak, Joe, *All About Victoria Square*, The Victorian Society, Birmingham Branch, 1989.

Hutton, William, *An History of Birmingham*, 2nd (1783) and 3rd (1795) Editions, Thomas Pearson, Birmingham, (2nd edition reprinted by EP Publishing in 1976).

Little, Bryan, *Birmingham Buildings: The Architectural Story of a Midland City*, David & Charles, Newton Abbot, 1971.

Pearson, J.M., *Canal Companion: Birmingham Canal Navigations*, J.M. Pearson and Associates, Burton-on-Trent, Staffs, 1989.

Pugh, Bridget and Crews, Anne, *Solid Citizens: Statues in Birmingham*, Westwood Press Publications, Sutton Coldfield, 1983.

Sidey, Tessa, *Public Art in Birmingham*, Birmingham Museums and Art Gallery, 1993.

Skipp, Victor, *A History of Greater Birmingham Down to 1830*, Victor Skipp, Yardley, Birmingham, 1980.

Skipp, Victor, *The Making of Victorian Birmingham*, Victor Skipp, Yardley, Birmingham, 1983.

Stephens, W.B. (ed.), *The Victoria History of the Counties of England*. vol VII: *The City of Birmingham*, Oxford University Press, 1964.

Sutcliffe, Anthony, and Smith, Roger, *History of Birmingham* vol III: *Birmingham 1939 - 1970*, Oxford University Press, 1974.

Tilson, Barbara (ed.), *Made in Birmingham: Design and Industry 1889 - 1989*, K.A.F. Brewin Books, Studley, Warwickshire, 1989.

The following books will also be of interest:

Cherry, Gordan, *Birmingham: A Study in Geography, History and Planning*, John Wiley, Chichester, 1994.

Gerard, AJ and Slater, TR (eds.), *Managing a Conurbation; Birmingham and its Region*, K.A.F. Brewin Books, Studley, 1996.

Chinn, Carl, *Birmingham: The Great Working City*, Birmingham City Council, 1994.

Upton, Chris, *A History of Birmingham*, Phillimore & Co., Chichester, 1993.

Index

A bold page number indicates a photograph